WRITING
ARCHETYPAL CHARACTER ARCS

The Hero's Journey and Beyond

WRITING ARCHETYPAL CHARACTER ARCS

The Hero's Journey and Beyond

K.M. WEILAND

Writing Archetypal Character Arcs

Copyright © 2023
K.M. Weiland

Cover design by Damonza.
Graphics in Chapter 8 by Sydney Watkins.

All rights reserved. No part of this publication may be reproduced, stored in a retrieval system, or transmitted in any form or by any means electronic, mechanical, photocopying, recording, or otherwise without the prior written permission of the publisher and copyright owner.

Published by PenForASword Publishing.

ISBN-13: 978-1-944936-14-3

TABLE OF CONTENTS

Introduction: Archetypal Character Arcs and the Search for Meaning 15

Part 1: The Six Life Arcs 23

Chapter 1: Introduction to the Six Archetypal Character Arcs 27
>The Six Archetypal Character Arcs of the Human Life
>The "Problem" With the Hero's Journey
>What Is an Archetypal Character Arc?
>Five Things to Know About Archetypal Character Arcs

Chapter 2: The Maiden Arc 39
>The Maiden Arc: Coming of Age
>Stakes: Individuating From the Tribe
>Antagonist: Facing the Predator and/or the Too-Good Mother
>Theme: Growing Into Potential, Power, and Responsibility
>Key Points of the Maiden Arc
>The Beats of the Maiden Arc
>Examples of the Maiden Arc

Chapter 3: The Hero Arc 55
>The Hero Arc: Slaying the Dragon
>Stakes: Leaving the Village to Save the Kingdom
>Antagonist: Facing the Status Quo
>Theme: Resolving the Need for Power and the Need for Love
>Key Points of the Hero Arc
>The Beats of the Hero Arc
>Examples of the Hero Arc

Chapter 4: The Queen Arc 69
>The Queen Arc: Defending the Kingdom
>Stakes: Accepting the Burden of Leadership
>Antagonist: The Empty Throne
>Theme: Power in Relationship
>Key Points of the Queen Arc

The Beats of the Queen Arc
Examples of the Queen Arc

Chapter 5: The King Arc 83
The King Arc: Becoming the Sacrifice
Stakes: Glimpsing the Beginning of the End
Antagonist: Confronting the Monsters at the Door
Theme: Sacrificing a King for a Kingdom
Key Points of the King Arc
The Beats of the King Arc
Examples of the King Arc

Chapter 6: The Crone Arc 97
The Crone Arc: Facing Down Death
Stakes: Literally Life and Death
Antagonist: Paying a Penny to the Ferryman
Theme: Choosing Descent and Return
Key Points of the Crone Arc
The Beats of the Crone Arc
Examples of the Crone Arc

Chapter 7: The Mage Arc 113
The Mage Arc: Joining God
Stakes: Leaving Behind a Good World for Those Who Follow
Antagonist: Understanding the Nature of Evil
Theme: Journeying On
Key Points of the Mage Arc
The Beats of the Mage Arc
Examples of the Mage Arc

Part 2: The Twelve Shadow Archetypes 125

Chapter 8: Introduction to the Twelve Shadow Archetypes 129
Twelve Shadow or Negative Archetypes
The Passive Counter-Archetypes
The Aggressive Counter-Archetypes
How the Shadow Archetypes Relate to the Thematic Truth/Lie
How the Shadow Archetypes Relate to the Positive Arcs

Chapter 9: Damsel and Vixen **139**
The Damsel: A Passive Refusal to Initiate Into Adulthood
The Damsel's Potential Arcs: Positive and Negative
The Vixen: A Manipulative/Aggressive Attempt to Avoid the Initiation Into Adulthood
The Vixen's Potential Arcs: Positive and Negative
Key Points of the Maiden's Shadow Archetypes
Examples of the Damsel and Vixen Archetypes

Chapter 10: Coward and Bully **149**
The Coward: A Passive Refusal to Take Responsibility
The Coward's Potential Arcs: Positive and Negative
The Bully: An Aggressive Refusal to Take Responsibility
The Bully's Potential Arcs: Positive and Negative
Key Points of the Hero's Shadow Archetypes
Examples of the Coward and Bully Archetypes

Chapter 11: Snow Queen and Sorceress **159**
The Snow Queen: A Passive Refusal to Fight for What She Loves
The Snow Queen's Potential Arcs: Positive and Negative
The Sorceress: An Aggressive Refusal to Do What Is Best for What She Loves
The Sorceress's Potential Arcs: Positive and Negative
Key Points of the Queen's Shadow Archetypes
Examples of the Snow Queen and Sorceress Archetypes

Chapter 12: Puppet and Tyrant **169**
The Coward: A Passive Refusal to Be a True Servant-Leader
The Puppet's Potential Arcs: Positive and Negative
The Tyrant: An Aggressive Refusal to Be a True Servant-Leader
The Tyrant's Potential Arcs: Positive and Negative
Key Points of the King's Shadow Archetypes
Examples of the Coward and Tyrant Archetypes

Chapter 13: Hermit and Witch **179**
The Hermit: A Passive Rejection of Both Life and Death
The Hermit's Potential Arcs: Positive and Negative

    The Wicked Witch: An Aggressive Rejection of Both Life and Death
    The Witch's Potential Arcs: Positive and Negative
    Key Points of the Crone's Shadow Archetypes
    Examples of the Hermit and Witch Archetypes

Chapter 14: Miser and Sorcerer 189
    The Miser: A Passive Hoarding of Power
    The Miser's Potential Arcs: Positive and Negative
    The Sorcerer: An Aggressive Hoarding of Power
    The Sorcerer's Potential Arcs: Positive and Negative
    Key Points of the Mage's Shadow Archetypes
    Examples of the Miser and Sorcerer Archetypes

Part 3: The Six Flat or Resting Archetypes 197

Chapter 15: Introduction to the Six Flat or Resting Archetypes 201
    Six Flat or "Resting" Archetypes
    How to use Flat Archetypes in a Story
    How the Positive Archetypes Relate to the Flat Archetypes
    How the Shadow Archetypes Relate to the Flat Archetypes

Chapter 16: The Child 211
    The Child Archetype: Untapped Potential
    The Child's Normal World
    The Child's Relationship to the Thematic Truth
    How the Child Creates Change in Supporting Characters
    Types of Stories That Feature a Child Protagonist
    Examples of the Child

Chapter 17: The Lover 221
    The Lover Archetype: Empowered Youth
    The Lover's Normal World
    The Lover's Relationship to the Thematic Truth
    How the Lover Creates Change in Supporting Characters
    Types of Stories That Feature a Lover Protagonist
    Examples of the Lover

Chapter 18: The Parent 231
   The Parent Archetype: The Hero at Home
   The Parent's Normal World
   The Parent's Relationship to the Thematic Truth
   How the Parent Creates Change in Supporting Characters
   Types of Stories That Feature a Parent Protagonist

Chapter 19: The Ruler 241
   The Ruler: True Sovereignty
   The Ruler's Normal World
   The Ruler's Relationship to the Thematic Truth
   How the Ruler Creates Change in Supporting Characters
   Types of Stories That Feature a Ruler Protagonist

Chapter 20: The Elder 249
   The Elder: Making Peace With Death
   The Elder's Normal World
   The Elder's Relationship to the Thematic Truth
   How the Elder Creates Change in Supporting Characters
   Types of Stories That Feature an Elder Protagonist

Chapter 21: The Mentor 259
   The Mentor: Coming Full Circle
   The Mentor's Normal World
   The Mentor's Relationship to the Thematic Truth
   How the Mentor Creates Change in Supporting Characters
   Types of Stories That Feature a Mentor Protagonist

Part 4: The Twelve Archetypal Antagonists 267

Chapter 22: Introduction to the Twelve Archetypal Antagonists 271
   What Is the Difference Between an Antagonist and an Antagonistic Force?
   Inner and Outer Antagonists
   Antagonists and Contagonists

Chapter 23: Authority and Predator 281
   The Maiden's Antagonists: Practical and Thematic

How the Maiden's Archetypal Antagonists Operate in the
Conflict and the Climactic Moment
Examples of the Authority and Predator Archetypes

Chapter 24: Dragon and Sick King 291
The Hero's Antagonists: Practical and Thematic
How the Hero's Archetypal Antagonists Operate in the
Conflict and the Climactic Moment
Examples of the Dragon and Sick King Archetypes

Chapter 25: Invader and Empty Throne 301
The Queen's Antagonists: Practical and Thematic
How the Queen's Archetypal Antagonists Operate in the
Conflict and the Climactic Moment
Examples of the Invader and Empty Throne Archetypes

Chapter 26: Cataclysm and Rebel 311
The King's Antagonists: Practical and Thematic
How the King's Archetypal Antagonists Operate in the
Conflict and the Climactic Moment
Examples of the Cataclysm and Rebel Archetypes

Chapter 27: Death Blight and Tempter 321
The Crone's Antagonists: Practical and Thematic
How the Crone's Archetypal Antagonists Operate in the
Conflict and the Climactic Moment
Examples of the Death Blight and Tempter Archetypes

Chapter 28: Evil and the Weakness of Humankind 331
The Mage's Antagonists: Practical and Thematic
How the Mage's Archetypal Antagonists Operate in the
Conflict and the Climactic Moment
Examples of Evil and the Weakness of Humankind as
Archetypes

Part 5: Practical Application of Archetypal Characters 339

Chapter 29: How to Use Archetypal Character Arcs in Your Story 343
Finding Your Own Character Archetypes

Remember, Archetypal Character Arcs Are Developmental, But Not Always Linear
Five Considerations for How to Use Archetypal Character Arcs

Appendix 1: Master List of the Archetypal Character Arcs 353
Overview of All Archetypes in the Life Cycle of Archetypal Character Arcs
Story Type for Each Archetype
Arc for Each Archetype
Symbolic Setting for Each Archetype
Thematic Lie vs. Truth for Each Archetype
Archetypal Antagonists for Each Arc
Archetypes' Positive Relationships to Own Shadow Archetypes
Archetypes' Potential Relationships to Subsequent Shadow Archetypes as Represented by Other Characters
Shadow Archetypes Overview

Appendix 2: How Story Structure and Archetypal Character Arcs Mirror Each Other 361
The Microcosm and the Macrocosm of Story Structure
First Act
Second Act
Third Act

"There are as many archetypes
as there are typical situations in life.
Endless repetition has engraved
these experiences into
our psychic constitution."
—C.G. Jung

Introduction

ARCHETYPAL CHARACTER ARCS AND THE SEARCH FOR MEANING

STORIES HAVE BEEN our constant companion throughout the journey of human existence. Why is that? Is it because they entertain us? Is it because they inform us? Because they distract us?

Yes, of course. But the very universality of, not just story itself, but our passionate connection to story would seem to indicate the human experience finds great resonance in the *act* of storytelling.

I do not think it too simplistic or idealistic a statement to say that storytelling is a quest for meaning. As creators and consumers of story (and, indeed, art as a whole), we all have personal connections to this. We often interact with stories, whether intellectually or emotionally, as a search for understanding. We turn to stories for catharsis, comfort, and catalytic challenge.

As writers, we gradually become more cognizant of this than even the average viewer or reader. As we study the craft and technique of writing, we eventually encounter humanity's collective ideas of story theory. These theories posit that there are certain patterns—which we generally identify by such terms as "story structure" and "character arc"—that repeat themselves over and over again to create the very definition (however loose) of what we consider a story at all.

When writers begin learning story theory principles, we often tend to identify them merely as "rules for success." But in recognizing that story itself is archetypal, these tools and techniques of the craft begin to emerge as a fascinating meta commentary on the deeper questions of life itself.

THE COSMOLOGY OF STORY THEORY

Before diving into the nitty-gritty of foundational archetypal characters and character arcs (including but going far beyond the prevalent Hero's Journey), I want to step back to the broader context. In Chapter 1, we'll be talking more specifically about actual archetypes in fiction. But first, I want to talk about story *itself* as archetype.

Several years ago at a time when I was particularly needing, searching for, and redefining meaning in my own life, I read Madeleine L'Engle's wonderful ode to the synthesis of art and spirit, *Walking on Water*. I resonated deeply with her notion of why it is that humans are driven to create and to tell stories. She recognized art as an ordering principle by which humankind strives to understand its own existence, referring to it by Carl Jung's phrase "cosmos in chaos." The more I study story theory, the more I have come to recognize it as something of a cosmology all its own—a microcosmic commentary on existence.

In short: an archetype.

What *is* an archetype? My dictionary offers three definitions:

1. A typical specimen.
2. An original model.
3. A universal or recurring symbol.

When what we write touches upon that which is archetypal (sometimes consciously, usually unconsciously), it is often surprisingly explicit in its ability to offer us answers and meaning in our questions about life.

For example, modern writers often tend to think of story structure as a format we *apply* to our stories. But, in fact, story structure is an *emergent*. It exists and it works—and we recognize it as such and try to engineer it into our own stories—because it reflects

WRITING ARCHETYPAL CHARACTER ARCS | 17

truthful patterns about life itself. The same is true, perhaps even more poignantly, for character arcs. For me, researching and writing my previous book *Creating Character Arcs* was a personally life-changing experience that provided insights far beyond writing. The reason character arcs resonate with us as readers and viewers is that they are *patterns within our own lives*.

And so it goes for even more "mythic" archetypal journeys, such as the Hero's Journey made so famous and ubiquitous by Joseph Campbell and George Lucas. These mythic story structures are endlessly repeatable because they *do* endlessly repeat in every single one of our lives.

Meanings, Patterns, Symbols, and Archetypes

Story theory is eminently practicable in supplying writers with techniques they can apply to improve the resonant power, and therefore success, of their stories. But this is really just a byproduct of the theory itself, which focuses on recognizing emergent patterns within our ever-growing body of stories. These patterns then contribute to our ability to recognize those particular symbols and archetypes that appear over and over again, almost universally, rising far above time, place, genre, or even thematic intention.

At their loftiest, the emergent patterns of human stories tell us something about all of existence. Usually, however, these patterns are most poignant when they help us tell our own stories, not just those we put on paper, but those we are living every moment of every day.

We may think of stories as something separate and apart from life itself, particularly in this day and age when stories are more accessible and abundant than ever and we most commonly interact with them with the intention of entertainment or distraction. But inevitably story is *not* separate. Indeed, perhaps the modern era has seen the line between story and reality grow more blurred and meta than ever. When we understand the symbiosis of art and life, we are able to simultaneously bring the patterns of life to the page and the patterns of the page to our lives.

Humans interact with stories for many reasons, all of them valid. But deeper than the entertainment, the distraction, or the titillation—deeper than the characters, the character arcs, and the plot structure—there is the resonance of story itself as a foundational archetypal reflection.

All art is necessarily both reflective and generative of the human experience. In that way, all art both reflects and generates archetype. Some stories do this more simply and obviously than others. Those stories that we recognize as myth or fable are most blatantly archetypal. But even hyper-realistic stories—when well done—offer up to us the archetypal truths of humanity.

Archetype: Story as Revelation

Many writers can speak to the experience of "receiving" a story. Much as Stephen King has famously described his own process, we don't so much create our stories as we discover them. It is as if the bones are always there, and all we have to do is figure out how to dig them up. When the creation process is at its most powerful, we are "in the zone," writing madly away, just hoping our fingers can move fast enough to get it all down before the inspiration fades.

When writers first begin learning about archetypal story structure, they are often astonished (as I was) to examine their own stories and discover that these archetypes they've never heard of before are there already within their best stories—or waiting to be uncovered to help those stories find a truer voice.

How is it that even the most uneducated writers seem to have at least a glimmer of an understanding for these archetypes? Perhaps it is because these patterns are everywhere, and we necessarily absorb them by osmosis. Perhaps, as the depth psychologists would have it, it is because these archetypes reside in a collective unconscious. Or perhaps it is simply because as humans, we resonate with the patterns of our existence and instinctively understand how to recreate them in our art.

WRITING ARCHETYPAL CHARACTER ARCS | 19

Whatever the case, archetypal stories and characters have populated the mythologies of the human experience for as long as we can remember. As Willa Cather says in one of my favorite quotes ever:

> There are only two or three human stories, and they go on repeating themselves as fiercely as if they never happened.

Mythological Character Archetypes

Most of what we specifically think of as character archetypes are found in the stories that have been mythologized, whether from history, religion, or folk and fairy tales. What we recognize as the origins for these stories and their characters are often simplistic, fantastical, and moralistic. They often repeat over and over again throughout the millennia, varied but always foundationally similar from culture to culture and era to era.

In *The Art of Fiction*, writing instructor John Gardner distinguished "fables," "yarns," and "tales" as layers of story that move increasingly away from non-reality (i.e., fantasy) into the more nuanced and specific realms of realism. But even hyper-realistic fiction rests upon the foundations of myth and its metaphors.

When modern writers think about archetype, we are most likely to think of the now ubiquitous Hero's Journey, made famous by Joseph Campbell's research of world myths in his book *The Hero With a Thousand Faces*. The Hero's Journey has since been codified by many writers (most notably Christopher Vogler in *The Writer's Journey*) as a profoundly powerful archetypal character arc.

Although the Hero's Journey is a deeply metaphoric structure that finds its most literal representation in the fantasy genre (with its often black-and-white representations of good and evil, complete with dragons, resurrections, kingdoms, and wizards), it proves its versatility by reappearing in story after story, both fantastical and realistic. It is not, however, the only archetypal character arc, and not even the most important one.

This is what we will discuss in this book, which centers around six primary and serial arcs (the Hero's Journey being the second).

Archetype as the Path to Powerful Stories

So why do archetypes matter? To a writer, they matter for the most obvious reason that they are stories. More than that, they are stories that *work*. The very fact that these patterns have stuck around over the years and proven themselves to still be meaningful should be enough to entice any writer. After all, that's what we're all hoping for in our own stories, isn't it?

Like the structure of plot and character itself, archetypes offer writers insights into modalities of deeper and more resonant fiction. The mere pattern of an archetype is not resonance in itself (as many cookie-cutter productions of the Hero's Journey, *ad nauseum*, have proven). But archetypes offer the storyteller a glimpse into some of the deeper insights and truths of humanity.

More than that, archetypes—particularly the specific archetypal character arcs that represent the human lifespan—have the potential to provide writers and readers a subconscious road map to our own initiatory journeys throughout our lives. That has been my own experience with these archetypal character arcs. Merely in coming to a recognition of them, I have found just as many gifts for myself as a person as I have as a writer.

Whether we are writing about falling in love in a YA novel, fighting dragons in a fantasy, making peace with adult children in contemporary fiction, ruling a corrupt dynasty in a historical novel, or conversing with the moon in magical realism—we are all writing about our own experiences of the world and, by extension, if we write well enough and truly enough, everyone else's experiences as well.

Part 1:
The Six Life Arcs

"Discovering who we are is a primary preoccupation of early adulthood. Life review, the affirmation of what our lives have meant, is a critical task of old age. In between is a journey in which our self-understanding grows insight by insight, day by day."
—Donald Maass

1

Introduction to the Six Archetypal Life Arcs

ARCHETYPAL STORIES ARE stories that transcend themselves. This is because archetypes speak to something larger. They are archetypal exactly because they are *too* large. They are larger than life. They are impossible—but ring with probability. They utilize a seeming representation of the finite as a mirror through which to glimpse infinitude.

Despite their almost numinous quality, archetypes are a very real force in our practical world. Think of it this way: *all the things we imagine actually exist.* Aliens. Vampires. Dragons. Fairies. All our memories of reality also exist—in real time—in the same way. Regardless whether these things can be proven as corporeal, they still exist within the human experience and impact it. The deeper the shared belief, the deeper and more meaningful the archetype becomes.

Stories are one of our most powerful modes of exploring archetypes. This is true in the very nature of story itself and more specifically in the patterns of plot and character arc structure that are revealed in the studies of story theory (which I've discussed in detail in my books *Structuring Your Novel* and *Creating Character Arcs*). Archetypes also show up in a legion of increasingly smaller ways—from genres to iconic character types to symbolic imagery. For a writer, one of the most exciting explorations of archetype can be found within *specific* character arcs—or journeys. These arcs have defined our literature throughout history, and they can be consciously used by any writer to strengthen plot, identify themes, explore life, and resonate with readers.

THE SIX ARCHETYPAL CHARACTER ARCS OF THE HUMAN LIFE

We already recognize that the arc of a story can be found reflected in smaller pieces of the whole. We see it on the level of scene structure, in which each scene creates a mini-story arc, complete with Inciting Event and Climax. We also certainly see it within the structure and arc of each individual act within an overall story. Indeed, each structural section, chapter, and beat ideally reflects this pattern.

We can also see this pattern projected out from story structure itself onto a larger domain. First, we may see the arc reflected from within a larger series (anything from the obvious three acts of a trilogy to a much longer series). But also, eventually, we can see it in life itself.

We will begin this book by exploring the six primary Positive Change character arcs of the "life cycle." They are:

1. The Maiden
2. The Hero
3. The Queen
4. The King
5. The Crone
6. The Mage

These archetypes are not random but sequential, marking out what we might see as the Three Acts of the human life. If we think of the average human life as lasting ninety years, then we can also think of that life in terms of Three Acts made up of roughly thirty years each.

> **The First Act**—or the first thirty years—is represented by the youthful arcs of the Maiden and the Hero and can be thought of thematically as a time of Individuation.

The Second Act—roughly years thirty to sixty—is represented by the mature arcs of the Queen and the King and can be thought of thematically as a time of Integration.

The Third Act—roughly years sixty to ninety—is represented by the elder arcs of the Crone and the Mage and can be thought of thematically as a time of Transcendence.

In her book *Women Who Run With the Wolves*, Clarissa Pinkola Estés, Ph.D., alludes to how these six archetypes (although she uses different names) are foundational to the human experience:

> The gardener, the king, and the magician are three mature personifications of the archetypal masculine. They correspond to the sacred trinity of the feminine personified by the maiden, mother, and crone.

For the purpose of our study, it is important to note that each of these six character arcs will build upon the previous ones to create the big picture of one single "life arc." The partner arcs within the same act are not interchangeable but distinct (i.e., the Maiden and the Hero are not simply gendered names for the same arc) and can be undertaken by any person of any gender (or even, potentially, any age).

Each of these archetypes represents a Positive Change Arc (such as I talk about more generally in *Creating Character Arcs*). In Part 2, we will also be examining the Negative Change Arcs represented by the passive/aggressive shadow archetypes for each type (e.g., the Bully and Coward as negative aspects of the Hero). Part 3 will cover the Flat Arc periods that exist *between* the Positive Change Arcs (e.g., the Elder as the interstitial archetype existing between the King Arc and the Crone Arc.). And finally, in Part 4, we will close with an examination of the internal and external archetypal antagonists that drive the conflict in each of the main six arcs (e.g., Invader and Empty Throne as antagonistic forces in the Queen Arc).

This perspective of the life arcs is certainly not the only archetypal system through which to view story or life. But it is an amazingly resonant tool for linking story structure to life and life to structure.

The "Problem" With the Hero's Journey

Although each of these six main archetypes is deeply familiar to us, only the Hero is noted for having a prominently recorded archetypal journey. Most writers these days are steeped in the mythology (both ancient and modern) and the canonized beatsheets of the Hero's Journey.

I can't speak specifically to every writer's relationship to the Hero's Journey, but I can speak to mine—which I daresay may indeed be similar to many people's. I grew up engulfed in the Hero's Journey, and I loved it. I resonated with it, played it out in the backyard with great gusto, and subconsciously recreated it in my own stories.

But then I started reading about it in writing guides... and I somehow didn't resonate with it quite as much. Even though its beats clearly lined up with classic structure, I couldn't help but feel a little claustrophobic about the idea that this was the *only* acceptable archetypal journey. Although many of the terms I now use in teaching story structure have been borrowed from the classic Hero's Journey, I have never specifically taught the Hero's Journey or even consciously tried to apply it to my own stories.

I always felt like something was missing. Then a few years ago, I read screenwriter Kim Hudson's *The Virgin's Promise*, which posits a feminine partner arc to the Hero's Journey. In the book, she reaffirmed Clarissa Pinkola Estés's point, above, about the Maiden and the Hero being merely the youthful archetypes, which should in a mature life be followed by the journeys of adulthood and elderhood.

In short, the Hero's Journey is *not* all-encompassing. It may be universal in the sense that it represents an archetypal pattern that shows up in all our lives. But it is only *one* of multiple important life arcs.

What not everyone realizes is that the microcosm of the Hero's Journey, as initially recorded by Joseph Campbell in his book *The Hero With a Thousand Faces*, represents the macrocosm of the entire life cycle of arcs. Campbell alludes to this in his original breakdown of the journey, and then dives into more depth in the book's final section, which goes beyond just the Hero's Journey as most of us have come to understand it. He uses different titles from those I've found most resonant for the life arcs, so I've included the terms I will be using in this book in brackets:

Transformations of the Hero:

1. The Primordial Hero and the Human [Child—initial Flat archetype]
2. Childhood of the Human Hero [Maiden Arc]
3. The Hero as Warrior [Hero Arc]
4. The Hero as Lover [Queen Arc]
5. The Hero as Emperor and as Tyrant [King Arc]
6. The Hero as World Redeemer [Crone Arc]
7. The Hero as Saint [Mage Arc]
8. Departure of the Hero [usually signified by Death]

Not only did the exemplary work of authors such as Estés, Hudson, and Campbell completely change how I view and plot my own stories, it also changed the way I view my life. Recognizing and studying these archetypes (and identifying which journey I am personally working on in my own life) has proven to be a profound initiatory experience.

Truly, *that* is the point of any good archetypal character arc.

What Is an Archetypal Character Arc?

If you have studied character arcs with me before, then you already know the essence of any character arc is change. Archetype adds the additional element of *changing the reader*—or at least, by its very nature, offering the opportunity for that change.

This is because all six of the archetypal arcs we will be discussing are initiatory arcs. By that, I mean they concern themselves on both a personal and symbolic scale with Life, Death, and Rebirth.

In short, archetypal arcs are not just about change. They are about change taken to its ultimate endpoint: what was can no longer be.

Of course, your story may or may not feature literal death; what is really meant here is that the arc of one archetype is fundamentally about its own death—and subsequent rebirth into the archetype that follows. For instance, the Maiden Arc is about the death of the Maiden archetype within the protagonist—and her rebirth into the Hero. The arcs are not about *becoming* the central archetypes (i.e., the Hero Arc is not about becoming a Hero), but rather about reaching the apotheosis of that archetype and then *transitioning out of* the height of that power into Death/Rebirth (i.e., the Hero surrenders his heroism and is reborn into a resting phase of the Queen archetype).

The foundational reason why these six arcs are so crucially central to the human experience is because they are *all* initiatory arcs. Particularly in our modern era when so many initiatory experiences (for the young, much less the adult and even less the elder) have been culturally lost or abandoned, these archetypal stories offer a deep resonant truth and even the subconscious guidance people crave.

Five Things to Know About Archetypal Character Arcs

In the next chapter, we will begin studying the structural beats and thematic significance of each of the arcs, starting with the Maiden Arc. However, before we dive into the specifics of each arc, I want to take a moment to discuss a few basic principles that apply to all the arcs.

1. Not All Stories Feature "Life Arc" Archetypes

Just as not every story features the Hero's Journey, not every story will necessarily feature *any* of these specific archetypal arcs. In my experience and study, most stories do fit into these categories, but just as these arcs are specific variations on the more general premises of the Positive Change Arc, Negative

Change Arc, and Flat Arc, there are also many variations on these archetypes.

2. These Archetypal Character Arcs Are Not the Only Archetypal Arcs

Archetypes are legion. Many systems exist for categorizing and naming character archetypes—everything from the Dramatica system to Jungian archetypes to the Enneagram. Almost all of them offer something valid and are worth studying and implementing. What I am exploring via these six Positive Change Arcs and their related Negative and Flat archetypes is simply one possible approach to character archetypes within your stories.

3. A Single Archetypal Character Arc Can Be Told Over the Course of Multiple Stories in a Series

Each of these character archetypes lends itself to a distinct and complete story structure, which can be used to plot a single book—and that is how we will be discussing them. But as all writers know, fiction itself isn't always so clear and cooperative. This means none of these archetypes *must* be confined to a single book. A character's journey through a single archetypal arc may, in fact, require multiple books or even an entire series to accomplish.

4. Multiple Archetypal Character Arcs Can Be Told in a Single Story

By the same token, it's possible (although much trickier) to combine multiple archetypes into a single larger character arc for a single character within a single book.

5. The Arcs Can Be Undertaken by Any Person of Any Gender or Age

As I mentioned earlier, these arcs can be undertaken by any person of any gender or age. For example, it is possible to see older characters undergoing a Hero's Journey. It is even possible to see how these experiences can be repeated within a smaller spiral of experience in *every chapter* of a human life. Indeed, the entire span of the arcs (from Maiden through Mage) can be seen mirrored within the individual structure of any one story. (For a thorough comparison of how the six life arcs mirror the beats of story structure, see Appendix 2 at the end of the book.)

Don't get hung up on the gendered titles of these arcs. I have retained these titles (Hero, Queen, etc.) precisely because they reflect the masculine and feminine aspects of the journey. But these titles do not indicate that the protagonist must correspondingly be male or female. For example, as is often discussed these days, characters taking a Hero's Journey need not be male.

More than that, every single one of these arcs is important, in its proper order, for *every* person, regardless of gender. Generally speaking, the feminine arcs begin in integration and move to individuation, while the masculine arcs begin in individuation and move back to integration. Both are necessary for wholeness and growth, each leading into the next.

"We are part of a finely balanced ecosystem in which interdependency goes hand-in-hand with individuation. We are all individuals, but we are also parts of a greater whole, united in something vast and beautiful beyond description."
—Michael Stark and Michael Washburn

2

THE MAIDEN ARC

THE FIRST ACT of the human experience—roughly the first thirty years—may be thought of as a period of Initiation. It is a period of integrating the parts of one's self.

As with all of the three periods that encompass these archetypal life arcs, the First Act is made up of two partner arcs, each leading into the other, each vitally important to mature development. The second of these arcs is perhaps the most popularly known of any archetypal character arc—the Hero Arc. But the Hero Arc cannot successfully launch the youthful person into adulthood unless it is founded upon the lessons learned from a completed Maiden Arc.

Because the Hero Arc is told almost to the complete exclusion (at least consciously) of the other life arcs, we don't find a wealth of study about writing these other arcs. This is a deep shame since it means both society and the individual misses out on the guidance of stories from other equally vital parts of life. It also means writers often feel they have but one primary model upon which to build stories. Instinctively, I think we all reject this—and yet where are the other models?

The answer is that at least some of them are now arising (or rather reemerging). The feminine arcs in particular are beginning to find voices. Within the last half century, more and more writers, psychologists, and social historians are offering models for these under-explored feminine arcs. I want to quickly reference some of these to indicate where I believe their models line up with the six life arcs I'll be talking about in this book. Some of the following books were written for writers, some not.

- First, we have Maureen Murdock's *The Heroine's Journey*—which I see as basically a female perspective on the Hero Arc.

- In her book *45 Master Characters*, Victoria Lynn Schmidt presents her own take on essentially the same approach as Murdock's.

- Recently, paranormal romance author Gail Carriger wrote a book also titled *The Heroine's Journey*. I see her discussion lining up nicely with the Queen Arc, which we'll explore in Chapter 4.

- And finally, screenwriter Kim Hudson's brilliant examination of the feminine counterpart to the Hero's Journey, which she calls *The Virgin's Promise*, equates with the Maiden Arc we are discussing in this chapter.

Aside from attributing some of the sources I've found invaluable and inspirational in studying this subject, I highlight this primarily to indicate there are *different* feminine arcs just as there are different masculine arcs. It's also worth noting there is often crossover in the models of these archetypal arcs and sometimes even in the arcs themselves. This is not an exact science. What I'm presenting in this book is simply what I've found rings true for me in my own life's journey and in writing my characters' journeys. As ever in all things story theory, you should always heed your own instincts (which understand archetypes much more deeply than any of our rational minds do anyway) in reconciling any parallels or inconsistencies.

THE MAIDEN ARC: COMING OF AGE

The Maiden Arc is the fundamental coming-of-age story. It is the story of a character who has left behind the Child archetype (which we will discuss in Chapter 16 when we reach the Flat

WRITING ARCHETYPAL CHARACTER ARCS | 41

Arc or "resting" archetypes), but who has not yet individuated away from her family and into her own autonomy.

The Maiden represents the awakening of sexuality and the burgeoning of consciousness. Hers is that fraught period—recreated in so many YA novels—when the person is learning who she will become and, perhaps most poignantly, what she is willing to risk to become that person.

There is no guarantee she will accept the risk. As with all of the arcs, there is no promise she will fully commit to and complete her arc. Although we all grow up physically and assume adult responsibility, the inner arc may remain uncompleted long into our lives. The obstacles the Maiden confronts are vast because true individuation is often perceived as a threat by the tribe in which she exists.

Stakes: Individuating From the Tribe

Because the Maiden is so young—just on the cusp of adulthood—she will still be perceived as a Child by her tribe. This is why the tribe is usually represented by her own family in some way. Symbolically, she has not yet ventured beyond the walls of her home. That home, which once seemed to be all the world, is now beginning to seem very small. The love of the parents, which once seemed so all-fulfilling, now begins to seem confining to her growth.

Inherent in this dilemma, we find the stakes of the Maiden Arc. The childhood life she has so far led is no longer proving to be enough for her—and so she must find the courage to risk giving it all up in some way (if only symbolically) in order to mature.

Antagonist: Facing the Predator and/or the Too-Good Mother

In the *Virgin's Promise*, Kim Hudson engineered a rock-solid exploration of this early arc of individuation, and I highly recommend her book for further study on this archetype. The beat sheet I'll be offering for the Maiden Arc later in this chapter, although influenced by Hudson's work, offers a varied approach.

In part, this is because I believe there is room within the concept of the Maiden Arc for several important archetypal antagonists, which Hudson does not directly discuss.

These antagonists are Authority and the Predator. Although these antagonistic forces may be literally represented within the story (and often are in fairy tales and fantasy), they can also be symbolically represented or can be presented for what they truly are: aspects of the Maiden's own psyche.

The Predator represents a toxic animus or masculine force within the Maiden. This is the part of her, whether externally represented in the conflict or not, that would destroy her from within by blocking her consciousness, her individuation, and her true empowerment. For example, Clarissa Pinkola Estés famously analyzed the Predator archetype in her retelling of the classic Bluebeard story about a Maiden who marries an older man and discovers all his previous wives murdered in a locked room.

Although the symbolic possibilities are endless, the Predator is often represented as a destructive or devouring force *apart* from the parents or Authority figures—and yet one to which, for "perfectly good" reasons, the parents often sacrifice the Maiden. Estés also comments on what she calls "the Too-Good Mother" and "the Naïve Father," from whom the Maiden must individuate in order to escape the Predator. Again, these are fundamentally internal antagonists within the Maiden herself, even when they are represented externally within the conflict.

One of my favorite examples of some of these archetypes is in the Cinderella adaptation *Ever After*, in which the protagonist is literally sold to a predatory old man because her naïve father married her devouring stepmother. A perhaps surprising example comes from the original *Terminator* movie (in so many ways a symbolic representation of the feminine journey to power), which externally represents both protagonist Sarah Connor's Predator and Protector. She eventually internalizes the power of the Protector (Kyle Reese) and destroys the Predator (the Terminator) herself.

(See Chapter 23 for a full exploration of the Maiden's archetypal antagonists.)

WRITING ARCHETYPAL CHARACTER ARCS | 43

Theme: Growing Into Potential, Power, and Responsibility

Although you may choose to represent the stakes in a Maiden Arc as life or death (as in *Terminator*), they are most literally represented within quiet coming-of-age stories that are simply about growing up. The challenge of the Maiden Arc is whether or not the protagonist will awaken to and accept her potential, power, and responsibility as an individual.

This may be represented by a character who is literally a child on the cusp of adolescence, such as Walter in the film *Secondhand Lions*. Or it may be represented by an adult who rejected this initiatory challenge at the proper time in his own life, such as the playboy protagonist in Nick Hornby's *About a Boy*.

The Maiden's story is foundationally one of a fight to empowerment. But whatever the external forces may be, it is foremost an internal struggle.

Will the Maiden be willing to let go of the carefreeness of childhood in exchange for the terrible freedom of adulthood?

Will she continue to cling to her own ignorance and naïvety? Her own blissful lack of consciousness?

Will she suppress her own instincts and desires, listening instead to the beguiling or threatening words of others?

Or will she rise up and confront the truth of Alice Walker's famous words?

> The most common way people give up their power is by thinking they don't have any.

KEY POINTS OF THE MAIDEN ARC

For easy reference and comparison, I will be sharing some scannable summations of each arc's key points.

Maiden's Story: An Initiation

Maiden Arc: Innocent to Individual (moves from Protected World to Real World)

Maiden's Symbolic Setting: Home

Maiden's Lie vs. Truth: Submission vs. Sovereignty

"Submission to authority figures is necessary for survival." versus "Personal sovereignty is necessary for growth and survival."

Maiden's Archetypal Antagonists: Authority/Predator (See Chapter 23)

Maiden's Relationship to Own Negative Shadow Archetypes:

Damsel finally owns her Potential by embracing her Strength.

Vixen learns to wield her true Potential with true Strength. (See Chapter 9)

Maiden's Relationship to Subsequent Shadow Archetypes as Represented by Other Characters: Potentially inspires Coward or outwits Bully. (See Chapter 10)

THE BEATS OF THE MAIDEN ARC

Following are structural beats for the Maiden Arc. I am using allegorical language in keeping with the tradition of the Hero's Journey (and honestly because it's so powerful). However, it is important to remember that the language is merely symbolic. Just as the Maiden need not actually be a "maiden" in any sense, neither do any of the other mentioned archetypes or settings need to be interpreted literally.

This is a general structure that can be used to recognize and strengthen Maiden Arcs in any type of story. Although I have interpreted the Maiden Arc through the beats of classic story structure, it doesn't necessarily have to line up this perfectly. A story can be a Maiden Arc without presenting all of these beats in exactly this order. For other interpretations of the Maiden's journey, check out some of the previously mentioned resources (especially Kim Hudson's *The Virgin's Promise*).

1ST ACT: Protected World

Beginning: Provided For But Unprepared

The Maiden lives still on the border of a seemingly blissful childhood. Even if all is not perfect in the home of her parents, she continues to experience a division between the perceived safety and providence of her childhood home and the dangerous—or at least unknown—world beyond.

But even as a part of her remains complacent in her ignorance of the larger world, change is beginning to stir within her, and this change is reflected outwardly as aspects of the "Real World" begin to slowly penetrate and change the Protected World of her childhood.

Up to this point in her life, the Maiden has been following the rules of her world for two reasons: to be rewarded by having her needs met and to avoid being punished. But the rules' requirements are beginning to cause her pain or constriction. The walls that are supposedly there to protect her are in fact preventing her from recognizing or defending herself against the Predator when he shows up.

> **For Example:** In *Bend It Like Beckham*, Jess lives at home with her parents, whom she loves but who do not understand or support her desire to play football (soccer).

Inciting Event: Predator's Proposal

The Maiden's quiet home world is interrupted by the arrival of a new force from beyond.

This force may be obviously a representation of the dangers her parents always warned her she wasn't capable of confronting.

Or it may disguise its danger with a mask of seduction that she is not yet wise enough to perceive.

Or this interruptive force may in fact be dangerous not so much literally but symbolically—in that the awakening of the Child into the adult world does indeed risk many dangers—as, for example, when the Maiden falls in love for the first time or is offered a "grown-up" opportunity.

Whatever the case, this Predator will seem to offer a way out of the restrictive world in which the Maiden is confined. He proposes to her—or perhaps instead to her parents. The Maiden herself isn't yet wise enough to recognize that the Predator is just a dangerous extension of the same power that rules her Protected World.

As symbolic extensions of her own naïvety, the Too-Good Mother and Naïve Father likewise do not see through the threat and/or are eager to accept the proposal for their own gain and/or at least do not see how to avoid sacrificing their daughter to save themselves.

> **For Example:** In a Maiden Arc, the love interest can represent the devouring Predator just as often as the Protector. In *Jane Eyre*, Mr. Rochester rather surprisingly represents the Predator. Even though he is redeemed in the end, he spends most of the story trying to bend Jane to his will in exchange for his love.

2ND ACT: Real World

First Plot Point: Inspired or Compelled to Fit New Identity; Protector Arrives

The Maiden accepts the Predator's proposal, either out of trust for her authority figures or out of her own true but misguided instinct to move forward into a larger consciousness. Whatever the case, she takes a first and irreversible step out of her childhood Protected World and into the Real World of the adults. In so doing, she spreads her wings for the first time and begins to experiment with new identities and desires.

No longer entirely confined by the rules and protection of her childhood, she dares to explore. Even though she is now the Predator's betrothed, she is still playacting, trying on this new role and believing she is maturing without realizing that she is still acting out the beliefs and expectations of others. However, she is also beginning to discover truths about herself: who she was and who she has the potential to become.

At this time, the Protector arrives. This may be in the form of a literal Protector of some kind (often a Hero), but it may also be simply the rising of the Maiden's own inner Protector—the healthy counterpart of the Predator. Even if a human Protector arrives (and even if he literally rescues her at some point in the story), he is not her savior. Whether a Lover or a Mentor, he represents a catalyst to prompt the inner change she herself must enact to reach autonomy.

> **For Example:** In *Secondhand Lions*, the young protagonist Walter finds surprising allies in his eccentric and cranky great-uncles, with whom his mother has abandoned him.

First Pinch Point: Predator Sees Through Disguise

The Maiden continues to explore her awakening consciousness into adulthood, but she does so in a sort of shadowland, avoiding the full awareness of those who remain back in her Protected World. Whether she is aware of the Predator's true and tyrannical nature, or whether she still partly believes in the seductive promise he seems to offer, she is becoming less and less subject to him—and therefore more and more threatened by what he offers.

As she secretly grows away from the identity he has assigned to her, he becomes suspicious and sees through her disguise. He recognizes she is not entirely a guileless, defenseless Maiden any longer but is on the cusp of breaking away from him. He will threaten or punish her in an attempt to bring her back under his power. She is deeply frightened, well aware of all she stands to lose if she departs her Protected World for good.

> **For Example:** In *Titanic*, Rose is reminded by both her predatory fiancé Cal and her desperate mother that the good of the family depends upon her marriage to a wealthy man she does not love.

Midpoint: Identities/Loyalties/Wants Conflict

A Moment of Truth arrives when the Maiden is confronted by the divide that has grown between who she used to be—and still tries to be—in the Protected World and who she is becoming in the Real World. Whether symbolically or literally, she is forced to confront the competing realities represented by the Predator and the Protector. She must choose which identity to internalize for the future.

She may do this by allying with an actual person representing the Protector, or merely symbolically by stepping into this role for herself and venturing into the Real World in an irrevocable way. She embraces her emerging self and the exciting Truth of who she has the potential to become, and she demonstrates true responsibility for her own choices in some significant way.

> **For Example:** In *Spirited Away*, Chihiro comes into her own by saving a river spirit. No longer just a clumsy, scared little girl, she proves she can hold her own amongst all the workers and guests at the bathhouse.

Second Pinch Point: Unmasked

Eventually, her choices and actions at the Midpoint are discovered, and she is unmasked. Her new identity fully emerges to everyone back in her Protected World. Whether well-meaning, controlling, or both, the people she has previously relied on are shocked by her transformation. Depending on their own symbolic roles, they may be threatened, grieved, or proud.

Regardless of their reactions, there are stakes to pay off. The Maiden's tribe will not fully relinquish her into the Real World without a struggle. There will be people who do not want her to change and leave, and these people will do whatever they can to keep her in the Protected World "for her own good."

> **For Example:** In *Ever After*, Danielle's step-family realizes she has been lying about her identity and spending time with the prince. They punish her by locking her in a cellar.

3ʳᴰ ACT

False Victory: Bride Price

The Predator returns with a more seductive or threatening offer than ever. He still wants his bride, and he is not willing to lose her. He ups the bride price and/or threatens the Maiden's family. Those around her beg her to consider what is best for the family that has always protected her. She herself is deeply conflicted. The stakes seem far too high. Can she really sacrifice everything she has ever loved—and perhaps her own survival—for the chance at this true life she has now glimpsed? She begins to think that perhaps this redoubled bride price is worth the exchange.

> **For Example:** In *Titanic*, Rose is given the chance to escape the sinking ship on a lifeboat, but only if she will leave her love Jack to die and return to the restrictive life she hates.

Third Plot Point: Marriage Treaty Threatened

The Maiden resists her impending enslavement to the Predator, and the Predator grows more and more threatening. The stakes rise, and her family's well-being appears to be at risk. Her once seemingly serene Protected World is now in an uproar. She withdraws and "wanders in the wilderness" (Hudson's term, which I love).

She is caught now between worlds, what Jean Shinoda Bolen in *Crossing to Avalon* calls the "labyrinth experience" of being "in the forest." She can never go back. Never again can she be the innocent, protected Child she once was. To sacrifice herself to the Predator, as her tribe demands, would be to turn her back on the burgeoning new self she has discovered and doom herself to an imprisoned half life—neither Child nor adult. To throw off the Predator and grow beyond the tribe also demands a life and death sacrifice, but only *this* death will offer the chance of a rebirth into something new.

> **For Example:** After fleeing her failed wedding to Rochester (when she discovered he was already married), Jane Eyre literally "wanders in the wilderness" to the point she nearly dies.

Climax: Fights Back Against Predator

Even right at the door of the church, the Maiden fights back against her marriage to the Predator. She will not surrender what she has discovered about herself and about life. She will not hide her newly won understanding of her own potential, power, and responsibility. She will fight. She will declare herself (in Jane Eyre's words) "a free human being with an independent will."

> **For Example:** In *Secondhand Lions*, Walter refuses to help his mother's abusive boyfriend steal his uncles' money. He stands up for them and fights back.

Climactic Moment: Comes of Age

The Maiden will triumph. She will overcome the Predator, perhaps with the help of the Protector and others whom she has inspired with her courage and independence, or perhaps alone, having internalized their support. If the Predator is truly evil, she will banish him forever from her family's home. If the Predator is representative only of the overprotective forces that would devour her out of misguided love, then she will at least attempt (and likely succeed) to make peace with them. She is an adult now—an equal—and she will treat others as such, receiving from them their respect in return.

> **For Example:** In *The Terminator*, Sarah watches Kyle (her externalized Protector) die for her. She internalizes his strength and the tactics he has taught her in order to save herself by destroying the predatory Terminator.

Resolution: Kingdom Is Renewed for Another Generation

Restrictive elements such as the Predator and negative Authority figures such as the Evil Stepmother will be cast off and banned from the Kingdom. Other characters who prove themselves willing to embrace and benefit from the Maiden's courageous growth will be renewed. By coming of age, she ensures the tribe will continue into a strong new generation.

> **For Example:** In the classic Bette Davis movie *Now, Voyager*, the once mousy and repressed heroine ends triumphantly transformed and ready to nurture the next generation.

WRITING ARCHETYPAL CHARACTER ARCS | 51

EXAMPLES OF THE MAIDEN ARC

Examples of the Maiden Arc include the following.

- Danielle de Barbarac in *Ever After*
- Will Freeman in *About a Boy*
- Walter Caldwell in *Secondhand Lions*
- Sarah Connor in *The Terminator*
- Jane Eyre in *Jane Eyre*
- Charlotte Vale in *Now, Voyager*
- Edward in *Edward Scissorhands*
- David Copperfield in the first part of *David Copperfield*
- Jess Bhamra in *Bend It Like Beckham*
- Javed Khan in *Blinded by the Light*
- Chihiro in *Spirited Away*
- Rose Dewitt Bukater in *Titanic*
- Truman Burbank in *The Truman Show*
- Winnie Foster in *Tuck, Everlasting*
- Rapunzel in *Tangled*
- Jo March in *Little Women*
- Neo in *The Matrix*
- Hiccup in *How to Train Your Dragon*
- Harvey Cheyne in *Captains Courageous*
- Todd Anderson in *Dead Poets Society*
- Sarah Williams in *Labyrinth*
- Betty Warren (and most of the other girls) in *Mona Lisa Smile*

"...to be brave without compassion,
generous without frugality,
prominent without humility:
this is fatal."
—Lao-tzu

3

THE HERO ARC

AH, THE HERO. Heroic stories are so important and so prevalent throughout the history of storytelling that the word "hero" itself has become all but synonymous with "protagonist." That the Hero Arc is, in fact, one of *many* important archetypal character arcs does not lessen its importance within the cycle.

The Hero's Journey came to popular consciousness in the last century with Joseph Campbell's exploration of the monomyth in *The Hero With a Thousand Faces*. The ideas in this book were famously utilized to create one of our most influential modern myths—George Lucas's *Star Wars*. Later, the ideas would be more explicitly codified as a tool specifically for writers, most notably in Christopher Vogler's *The Writer's Journey*. Writers, viewers, and readers alike have clamorously embraced the Hero's Journey for the obvious reason that it resonates and resonates deeply.

However, in more recent years, the Hero's Journey has come under scrutiny for a number of reasons, including:

- Over-emphasizing masculine agency at the expense of feminine agency.
- Creating problematic social narratives around violence, saviorism, and narcissism.

- Indicating that it is the only—or at least the best—model for structuring a story.

These are all valid criticisms, but I find most of them arise out of the simple problem that the Hero's Journey has been asked to hold the spotlight alone, without reference to the other equally vital archetypal character arcs that can be seen to define the human life.

The Hero Arc is primarily a character arc of initiation. Although it can be taken (or re-taken) by people later in life (particularly if they failed to properly fulfill the arc's lessons in their younger years), the Hero Arc is one of the two "youthful" arcs belonging to the First Act of the human life, or approximately its first thirty years.

As we discussed in the last chapter, the first of these youthful archetypes is that of the Maiden, a coming-of-age arc that lays the foundation for the independent questing of the Hero. The Hero Arc then finishes the early initiatory phase of the First Act by asking the protagonist to complete his individuation and reach a level of maturity that allows him to reintegrate with the larger tribe or Kingdom as an adult.

If the Maiden Arc is about claiming one's personal power, the Hero Arc is about learning to use that power in service to a greater good. The Hero's challenge is that of arcing into the great responsibility of midlife.

THE HERO ARC: SLAYING THE DRAGON

The Hero Arc is the story of the conquering champion—the ingenuous but perhaps immodest youth setting out to accomplish a great feat that seems far out of his reach. He does the deed—he slays the Dragon—heals the sick old King—rescues the fair lady—saves the Kingdom. But in the end he does it not for glory but for love.

Throughout his adventures the Hero grows in experience and wisdom, often guided by a Mentor, which is the Flat Arc form of the Mage archetype (both of which we will be discussing in later chapters). The Hero will be tempted by his own

WRITING ARCHETYPAL CHARACTER ARCS | 57

growing power over the material world (sometimes symbolized by actual magical powers), but if he is to successfully avoid falling into the negative archetypes that constantly shadow him—the Coward and the Bully—he must eventually reach a new perspective and with it a willingness to sacrifice himself in defense of those he loves and who are worthy.

It is interesting that the classic Hero's Journey is not only about utilizing youthful power to slay the antagonistic Dragon, but also about *returning* to the village with the healing elixir.

In short: it is love that brings him back.

Stakes: Leaving the Village to Save the Kingdom

The Hero's Journey is often called the Hero's Quest. It is necessarily defined by some sort of journey, often literal but also sometimes metaphorical.

The young Hero, newly awakened to his individuality and growing independence, is compelled to leave behind his village in order to undertake an important quest. What he will find at the end will ultimately be his own maturity and his ability to return to the Kingdom. More symbolically, what he will find is the "elixir" that will heal the wounded Kingdom.

The Hero's departure from his home into "a larger world" is important because it symbolizes his complete and final separation and individuation from the tribe. What follows is his true test and initiation into adulthood. As such, even if he gathers companions on the road, the adventure is one that emphasizes his aloneness, which is often represented via his "specialness" in some way.

Antagonist: Facing the Status Quo

The antagonist in the Hero Arc is almost always externalized. It is something or someone—symbolized as the mindless, greedy, ever-devouring Dragon—that causes unhealth in the Kingdom and creates obstacles between the Hero and his ability to claim the healing elixir.

Campbell additionally portrays this deeply archetypal initiatory antagonist as the social "status quo"—or the tyrant "Holdfast, the keeper of the past"—the Sick King against which the emerging individual must prove he is willing and able to stand.

Although the Hero may begin the story already chafing against his village's stultifying confines (the poisonous effects of Holdfast), he will usually be at least somewhat reluctant to fully undertake his Quest. We speak of this as the Refusal of the Call—a beat that follows the Inciting Event halfway through the First Act. This refusal, whether represented by the Hero's own reluctance or someone else's on his behalf, emphasizes all the reasons the Hero might be better off *not* taking up the challenge of leaving the protection of tribe and village in order to become a fully individuated and independent adult.

After all, as illustrated potently in *Spider-Man*:

> With great power comes great responsibility.

In many ways, that is a succinct summary of the challenges of every Hero Arc.

(See Chapter 24 for a full exploration of the Hero's archetypal antagonists.)

Theme: Resolving the Need for Power and the Need for Love

As an emerging adult, the Hero is on the brink of discovering his great power. This discovery is vital to his maturation, but it is also a dangerous challenge. The Hero's power, should it ever grow unchecked, will be as great a threat to his own Kingdom as is the Dragon he now faces.

Therefore, the deep internal challenge of the Hero Arc is about reconciling his need and ability for power with his need and ability for love. As he grows in power throughout the journey, he will be given many opportunities to use it in his own favor and at the expense of others. If he is to positively complete his initiation into true and mature adulthood, he must face his own *inner* dragons and evolve into the even more potent (and frightening) power of love.

Although the Hero's particular manifestation of love is

about serving something greater and reintegrating into society in order to do so, his love is often represented specifically through a *love interest* character. This character may be used to teach him about love and to demonstrate his capacity to sacrifice for something greater in the end. Although the "damsel in distress" trope is widely criticized these days for contributing to a flawed social narrative, it's worthwhile to understand that, as with all stories, the archetypal underpinnings can be seen to represent different aspects of a single psyche. In other words, within our own Hero Arcs in our own lives, we can recognize that the damsel we, as Hero, rescue is in fact just another part of ourselves.

Key Points of the Hero Arc

Hero's Story: A Quest

Hero Arc: Individual to Protector (moves from Normal World to Adventure World)

Hero's Symbolic Setting: Village

Hero's Lie vs. Truth: Complacency and/or Recklessness vs. Courage

> "My actions are insignificant in the overall scope of the world." versus "All my actions affect those I love."

Hero's Archetypal Antagonists: Dragon and Sick King (see Chapter 24)

Hero's Relationship to Own Negative Shadow Archetypes:

Coward finally uses his Strength because he learns to Love and wants to defend what he loves.

Bully learns to submit his Strength to the service of Love. (See Chapter 10)

Hero's Relationship to Subsequent Shadow Archetypes as Represented by Other Characters: Potentially rescues Snow Queen or releases Sorceress with his love. (See Chapter 11)

The Beats of the Hero Arc

Following are structural beats for the Hero Arc. This is a general structure that can be used to recognize and strengthen Hero Arcs in any type of story. For the most part what follows is in line with Campbell's (and Vogler's) traditional Hero's Journey.

1ST ACT: Normal World

Beginning: Complacent But Unfulfilled

The Hero is a relatively mature young adult. He has awakened to his own adulthood and taken his place among the other adults in his village, but he chafes against the *normality* of it all. He has yet to try his wings or gain any real experience in the wider world. Before him stretches an unending road in which his life seems mapped out for him as he follows faithfully in the footsteps of all those who have come before.

And yet he does not choose to leave. He does not quite know *how* to leave, and deep down in the remnants of his Child heart, he retains fears of what it would mean to step beyond the comparative safety of his Normal World. This, however, is an illusion, because all is not well in the Kingdom. Even if the destruction has not yet reached his particular village, rumors abound: the Dragon is threatening.

> **For Example:** In *Star Wars: A New Hope*, Luke Skywalker pines for a more exciting life, away from his uncle's farm. He says he "hates" the Empire but feels little of its effects and isn't yet motivated to personally face its oppression.

Inciting Event: Call to Adventure

For what might seem like the first time in the Hero's entire life *something happens*. A stranger comes to town and/or the Hero makes a strange discovery. Though his tribal training and his fellow villagers tell him to leave it alone, his curiosity gets the better of him. He engages himself with this new occurrence in an irrevocable way.

He may act thoughtlessly with no real intent of getting involved, but he soon realizes he *is* involved. He is presented

WRITING ARCHETYPAL CHARACTER ARCS | 61

with a Call to Adventure that suggests he must go out on the road to complete an important quest in service to the Kingdom's great need. For one reason or another, he attempts to reject this Call. The complacency of "what has always been" tries to keep him in the village.

> **For Example:** In *The Wizard of Oz*, Dorothy Gale is unwillingly trapped by a tornado, which will carry her "over the rainbow" to her Adventure World in Oz.

2ND ACT: Adventure World

First Plot Point: Crosses the Threshold

The destruction now reaches the village in an undeniable way. The Kingdom's problems cease to be theoretical and become irrevocably personal to the Hero. It may be that someone he loves is injured or killed, or the village itself comes under attack. Whatever the case, the Hero walks through a Door of No Return—crosses its threshold—and leaves behind his village.

The adventure he has always craved has now begun. Even if he bears great sorrow for whatever catalyst forced him from the village, a part of him is excited by the prospects that now await him. He feels his power growing within, and he begins to explore himself beyond the limitations the village always set upon him. His intentions in aiding the Kingdom are good—pure-hearted—but his understanding of power dynamics is immature. He has no idea what he is getting himself into as he slowly begins to adopt the identity of Hero.

> **For Example:** In *Spider-Man* (2002), Peter Parker's life is radically changed when he witnesses (and is partially responsible for) his beloved uncle's murder.

First Pinch Point: Motives and Actions Questioned: "Who Do You Think You Are?"

He is brought up against his own limitations when his hubristic actions receive push-back from others. Mentors, allies, and love interests may caution him or express concern over his heedless actions. But he will also likely receive some sort of check from the antagonist or the antagonist's proxies.

All of his motives and actions up to this point in the quest are put under scrutiny. He is asked, contemptuously, "Who do you think you are?"

The truth is, he thinks himself quite a lot—a Hero, thank you very much. But this setback forces him to contemplate a different answer. The truth is he doesn't know who he is at all. He's not really a Hero. So far, he's just been playing at being one.

> **For Example:** In *Treasure Planet*, Jim Hawkins feels he failed after a crew member ostensibly dies because of him. Everyone, including himself, questions the progress he has made aboard ship.

Midpoint: "Remembering" Who He Is

The doubts raised in the previous beat come to a head as the Hero opposes the antagonist in a significant way. The outcome is ambiguous—in some ways a defeat, in others a victory. Most importantly, it offers a Moment of Truth that gives him great insight into how he might more effectively oppose the antagonist in the external conflict, as well as a glimpse into the glorious truth of his own identity.

He *is* a Hero. He is an individual. He is powerful. He glimpses his true potential and begins claiming his true power.

But he hasn't yet conquered his shadows. A tendency toward grandiosity remains, along with the subtle lure of absolute power's many temptations. Even as those he loves applaud his growing heroism, their doubts remain. The good-hearted boy who started this quest is growing into a powerful man. How he will ultimately use that power remains to be seen.

> **For Example:** In *Thor*, the Midpoint dramatically reminds the protagonist of his hubris and that "who he is" is someone not currently worthy to raise the mythical hammer Mjolnir.

Second Pinch Point: Betrayal: "It's All Your Fault"

The Hero experiences a betrayal of some sort by someone he trusted—whether an ally or an enemy in disguise. Despite all his good intentions, he is blamed for a setback in the quest to obtain the elixir. This accusation may be the direct result of his own culpable mistake. Or it may instead be the result of someone else's resentment toward his carelessness or arrogance earlier in the quest. Regardless, it is a blow that both sets back his pursuit of the elixir and forces him into a deeper contemplation of his own values.

> **For Example:** In *Far & Away*, Irish emigrant Joseph Donnelly loses an important boxing match when he tries to protect his love interest Shannon. Their crime-lord boss fires them, casting them out onto the street.

3RD ACT

False Victory: Means, Not Ends

As stakes rise in the Kingdom's plight, the Hero executes a desperate gambit to finally defeat the Dragon and steal away the elixir. He gains a victory but compromises all he has learned so far in order to do it. He chooses false means in order to achieve his end—and the victory rings hollow as a result.

> **For Example:** In *The Hunger Games*, Katniss Everdeen embraces the lie that she is romantically involved with her fellow competitor Peeta in hopes they both can survive the game, only to have the hope reversed later on.

Third Plot Point: All Is Lost

As a result of his own mistake, the Hero suffers a great loss or wound. It seems all is lost. Death is everywhere. The Hero may lose someone he loves, either directly as a result of his own mistake or because this person sacrifices to correct the problem. It is also possible the Hero may literally or symbolically pay for his mistake with his own life.

Regardless how the symbolism manifests, he is forced to confront a life and death choice—probably literally but certainly internally. He must choose whether he is willing to let die the immature, power-hungry boy he once was. The time has come when he must once and for all face the choice between power and love—so that he might integrate them.

> **For Example:** Thor sacrifices himself to his brother's wrath in order to save others, and he seemingly dies.

Climax: Resurrection

Because this is a Positive Change Arc, the Hero will choose rightly. He will choose life, and he will choose love. Symbolically (and in some stories literally), he will resurrect. The battle seemed irrevocably lost, but as he rises, the tide turns. The death he faced in the previous beat was not one he faced willingly, but having found meaning in the idea of sacrificing himself for the greater good of those he loves, he now willingly faces the possibility of true death.

> **For Example:** In *Mulan*, the protagonist "resurrects" into her true identity as both a woman and a warrior in order to confront the antagonist in the Climax.

Climactic Moment: Dragon Vanquished

The Hero's inner transformation represents the symbolic destruction of the Dragon's presence as a tyrannical power. However, the Hero must still defeat the Dragon literally in order to remove destruction from the Kingdom, either directly or by subsequently claiming his reward of the elixir. It is always possible the Hero might indeed give his life and die to achieve this end. But traditionally, since this archetype is not the end of the larger story, the Hero will emerge triumphant.

> **For Example:** Luke Skywalker destroys the Death Star.

Resolution: Kingdom at Peace

He returns to restore the Kingdom with the elixir. He may return to his village, ready to truly take his place as a fully initiated adult. But more symbolically, he will be elevated to a new rank and take on greater responsibility in helping to run the Kingdom itself.

> **For Example:** At the end of *Back to the Future*, Marty McFly returns home to discover that his adventures in the past have completely redeemed and "healed" his family.

EXAMPLES OF THE HERO ARC

Examples of the Hero Arc include the following.

- Luke Skywalker in *Star Wars*
- Mulan in *Mulan*
- Dorothy Gale in *The Wizard of Oz*
- Peter Parker in *Spider-Man*
- Jim Hawkins in *Treasure Planet*
- Katniss Everdeen in *The Hunger Games*
- Thor Odinson in *Thor*
- Marty McFly in *Back to the Future*
- Joseph Donnelly and Shannon Christie in *Far & Away*
- Mikey in *The Goonies*
- Evie Carnahan in *The Mummy*
- Simba in *The Lion King*

"The benevolent Queen uses her authority
to protect those in her court
and sees her own empowerment enhanced
by her relationships and experience."
—Caroline Myss

4

THE QUEEN ARC

WHAT HAPPENS AFTER the happily ever after? This is a question we often ask but don't always explore. As discussed in previous chapters, the two archetypal character arcs that begin the cycle of the six life arcs are the Maiden and the Hero. Together, they account for a great majority of the archetypal stories we read and view, and together they act to resolve the protagonist's initiation into adulthood—which often ends "happily" with the protagonist's reintegration into a meaningful position of work and relationship within the larger tribe or Kingdom.

But the vague "ever after" part of the phrase is only there if we choose not to follow the character into the life arcs of the Second Act of her life. Just as the two arcs of the First Act were characterized as representing the first thirty years of the character's life, the next two arcs can be thought of as representing the Second Act and comprising the next thirty years—approximately from the ages of thirty to sixty.

What we see represented here is a more mature phase of life—an unequivocally adult phase. The protagonist has put behind her the challenges of individuation and initiation on her way to discovering healthy relationships, building her own family, and investing herself in meaningful work. But as anyone who is chronologically in the Second Act can attest, the adventure is far from over.

If the overarching theme/challenge of the First Act was Fear, that of the Second Act is Power. The Queen Arc, particularly, is an arc about learning to accept and use one's power in relationship and in authority. After returning from the Hero's adventures of the quest, the initiated adult has settled down and started a family, whether literally or symbolically, which is why the static archetype that lives between the Hero and the Queen is that of the Parent (as discussed in Chapter 18).

However, the love the Hero learned in his arc is no longer enough to bear up the Queen's growing burdens of responsibility. If she is to continue her maturation and evolve her abilities to defend, enable, and direct the next generation of Maidens and Heroes in their own journeys, then she must grow *beyond* the role of loving Parent into the true leadership of the subsequent static archetype of the Ruler—and its following arc of the King.

For me personally, the Queen Arc has been one of the most exciting to recognize. In exploring sequels to my own novels, I was challenged to ask what we all ask sooner or later, "What happens to the Hero after the Hero's Journey?" Is it just *another* Hero's Journey? Instinctively, I think we all know true characterization demands that the sequel for any Hero must offer an even deeper journey into the protagonist's self. That journey is the Queen Arc.

THE QUEEN ARC: DEFENDING THE KINGDOM

The Queen represents who the Hero grows into after returning from the quest. She represents not just someone with the capacity for heroism, but also someone with a deep connection to and compassion for those she previously saved, for her family and community.

That community—her Domestic World—is a rich and joyous place, full of love and nurturing, where she has found purpose and joy in guiding the Children and directing the Maidens. But it is easy for her to lose herself at the hearth, so to speak, in this loving world and the headiness of having so many adoring dependents—her children (literal or metaphorical) with whom she deeply identifies.

Fortunately, as in all transformative stories, a catalyst arrives to prompt her growth into the next phase of her life (and her children into theirs). The Kingdom comes under threat from outside forces, and the current leadership proves itself incapable of protecting her family.

Whatever is a Queen to do?

Stakes: Accepting the Burden of Leadership

The Hero, in the previous arc, had to realize that love creates meaning, but the Queen must now recognize that love isn't enough. There must also be order, else all is chaos: the children will all be spoiled brats who never leave their mother's breast, never graduate from Maiden to Hero.

But there is a tremendous part of her that cannot bear that her children should grow up and leave her. Like all the positive archetypes, she stands on the narrow center point between her negative shadow poles—the Snow Queen and the Sorceress, who not coincidentally are often the villainous representations of corrupted power in Maiden Arcs. In order to successfully fulfill her next growth arc, the Queen is now required to mature *away* from her own needs for connection. She must mature into the comparatively lonely role of a leader, willing to entrust responsibility to her able subordinates. Part of her challenge in arcing into a Ruler is letting her children grow up. Because she enjoys being Queen, she doesn't necessarily want to be a Ruler. Relinquishing her children feels like a death and indeed, symbolically, is.

Unlike the Maiden and Hero, who resist their incumbent evolution out of fear of the powers that be, the Queen resists change because she is content. She likes where she is and feels she's earned it. And yet, necessity calls. Her brood grows too big. They require guidance. They need to be released from the home into the Kingdom and beyond. The Queen must transform and rise up to face the threats against the Kingdom by becoming the leader the Kingdom needs. Her love must grow from enveloping and protecting to enabling and ordering.

Her fear of becoming a Ruler isn't because she lacks the necessary qualities—power, will, intelligence. Her fear is that in giving up on her Queen identity, she can no longer be identified with her children—or they with her. No longer can she throw herself in front of a wayward child and tell the punisher—"Take me instead." Now she must view her children as subjects and become, instead of their shield, an impartial arbiter.

Antagonist: The Empty Throne

The catalyst that drives the Queen into action and growth is represented by an exterior threat to the Kingdom. Invaders are threatening at the borders. However, the true antagonist within her story is the Kingdom's lack of a mature and healthy leader to combat this threat. The Queen will start out appealing to what leadership exists, only to discover the throne is, symbolically, empty. It is occupied by either a Puppet or a Tyrant, who presents as great a threat to the Kingdom from within as does the Invader from without.

Despite her initial attempts and desires to work within the existing system, the Queen must eventually realize the only way to protect her children is to rise up and do it herself. She does this not out of a personal need (as does the Maiden) or a desire for glory (as does the Hero), but purely in defense of what she loves.

(See Chapter 25 for a full exploration of the Queen's archetypal antagonists.)

Theme: Power in Relationship

The Maiden and Hero Arcs evolve the character into personal responsibility. The Queen Arc and later the King Arc demand the character evolve into relational and social responsibility. No matter what "invasion" may be threatening in the story's outer conflict, this evolution into leadership is the central thematic focus of the Queen Arc.

Once again, it's important to note that the language used

WRITING ARCHETYPAL CHARACTER ARCS | 73

throughout this book is by nature archetypal. We speak of Queens and Kingdoms and Invaders and Thrones, but these concepts can be represented just as immediately in contemporary stories with none of these trappings.

One of my favorite examples of the Queen Arc is the baseball comedy *A League of Their Own*, which takes place against the backdrop of the All-American Girls Professional Baseball League during World War II. In it, the protagonist Dottie (played by Geena Davis) reluctantly undertakes a Queen Arc, growing into mature leadership, cleverly outmaneuvering the threats from without that would shut down the league and the threats from poor leadership within (the alcoholic, apathetic manager played by Tom Hanks). Eventually, she demands individual responsibility from her "subjects"—the other players and particularly her Maiden-archetype younger sister.

Unlike the Hero, who in order to properly fulfill his growth challenges must win alone, the Queen's growth arc demands she enable others to work with her. She will start out in a more Hero-appropriate mindset, wanting to do it the way she did it before and spare everyone else the conflict, but she must learn that she cannot—that she is only able to save her family by enabling them to take up arms alongside her.

Key Points of the Queen Arc

Queen's Story: A Battle

Queen Arc: Protector to Leader (moves from Domestic World to Monarchic World)

Queen's Symbolic Setting: Kingdom

Queen's Lie vs. Truth: Control vs. Leadership

> "Only my loving control can protect those I love." versus "Only wise leadership and trust in those I love can protect them and allow us all to grow."

Queen's Archetypal Antagonists: Invader and Empty Throne (see Chapter 25)

Queen's Relationship to Own Negative Shadow Archetypes:

Snow Queen finally acts in Love for her children by accepting Responsibility.

Sorceress learns to submit her selfish Love to the greater love of Responsibility. (See Chapter 11)

Queen's Relationship to Subsequent Shadow Archetypes as Represented by Other Characters: Potentially empowers Puppet or overcomes Tyrant with her power. (See Chapter 12)

THE BEATS OF THE QUEEN ARC

Following are general structural beats for the Queen Arc. (Check out *The Heroine's Journey* by Gail Carriger for an approach that is similar to the Queen Arc in many ways.)

1ST ACT: Domestic World

Beginning: Dangers of Dependency

The Queen is busy and fulfilled, caring for her growing children. She is, however, in danger of identifying herself too much with her children's dependency upon her and therefore of binding her children to her too tightly instead of allowing them to grow up and individuate via their own Maiden Arcs.

> **For Example:** In the beginning of *Places in the Heart*, before her husband is accidentally killed, Edna is content in her happy home as mother to her two children.

Inciting Event: Enemies at the Door

The Domestic World is threatened when enemies arrive from "without." Unfortunately, there is no one fit to defend the Kingdom from these Invaders. It could be there is no King, or the King is incompetent and/or corrupt, or the current King is arcing into an Elder and recognizes he must name and train a successor.

Whatever the case, the King will prove unwilling or unable to defend the Kingdom from the Invaders, and the Queen's realm will be threatened by this void of leadership. This "Call to Leadership" will be countered by a Refusal of the Call when the Queen resists immediately taking charge of her family's defense and instead chooses to believe she can convince the existing King to do what is necessary.

> **For Example:** In *Gladiator*, when an aging Emperor Marcus Aurelius entreats his famous general Maximus to rule Rome after his passing, in order to protect it from his psychopathic son Commodus, Maximus refuses, desiring instead to return to his wife and son on his farm in Spain.

2ND ACT: Monarchic World
First Plot Point: Entering the Castle

In order to entreat the King, the Queen reluctantly leaves her beloved Domestic World and enters the Monarchic World of the castle. She demands from him protection for her children. She may not immediately despair of the King's ability to defend the Kingdom, but she does realize that she must do something herself even if it is at the bidding of the King (who is either trying to fob off his own responsibility onto her or simply fob *her* off).

> **For Example:** In *Elizabeth*, the protagonist Elizabeth I is crowned Queen of England, but she is not yet truly the ruler of her people. Her advisers rule the country and will not allow her to wield true power.

First Pinch Point: Children Clamor for Action

The Queen's children aren't content with her diplomatic attempts to assure their safety against the enemy. They believe in their mother more than they believe in the King, and they want her to take charge and help them defend the hearth and home she has taught them to believe in and cherish. She resists this, neither wanting to leave her family to sit upon the throne, nor wanting her children to take up arms on her behalf. She continues to hope and work for the King's enablement against the Invaders.

For Example: In *The Order of the Phoenix*, Harry Potter secretly begins teaching other students, at their insistence, so they can form "Dumbledore's Army" and resist Voldemort (the Invader) and Professor Umbridge (a Tyrant representing the Empty Throne).

Midpoint: Leading the Charge

Finally, the Queen finds herself with no choice but to take charge and assume leadership in pushing back the Invaders. She comes to a Moment of Truth in realizing her love alone is not enough to protect her children. More than that, she cannot rely on others (i.e., the King) to perform the necessary acts of restoring order to the Kingdom. But neither can she win alone; she must lead a charge made up of her subjects. With some reluctance, she agrees to lead her children to battle.

The children wish to fight for their mother and put her upon the throne, but they also begin to fear that her growing power will trap them in childhood (as it will if she fails to arc into the King and instead slides into one of the negative archetypes of Snow Queen or Sorceress). If she fails to let them fight with her, as they demand, then she becomes an obstacle to their growth into adulthood. Only if she signals her own increasing shift into true leadership by challenging them to grow up and to fight behind her, will she signify that her Queen/Mother aspect will no longer hold them back. Indeed, her actions here not only signal her own shift from Queen toward King, but also demand that her children begin shifting from Maidens to Heroes.

For Example: In *A League of Their Own*, when the baseball players learn their league is struggling, Dottie leads the charge with theatrical stunts that bring in crowds, inspiring the other women to do the same.

Second Pinch Point: Children Become Adults

The children, in part inspired by the Queen's example so far and in part galvanized by her remaining hesitancy, individuate from her. They wish to take responsibility for their own lives,

WRITING ARCHETYPAL CHARACTER ARCS | 77

to become subjects rather than children (although they do not yet fully understand the weight of this choice). They insist she must claim the throne, even though this may mean she will eventually have to start meting out impartial punishment to some of them to maintain order.

> **For Example:** In *Elizabeth*, the queen demands her long-time love Lord Robert "grow up" and take responsibility for his own foolishness and his role as her subject.

3RD ACT

False Victory: Protects Her Children

The Queen makes a deal that protects her children, but it is at the expense of their independence. It represents a failure of leadership, in that she moves between negative archetypes—both the fearful and possessive "love" of the Sorceress and the total control of the Tyrant.

> **For Example:** In *It's a Wonderful Life*, George Bailey tries to bear the sole burden for the money his business partner has lost. Instead of asking his friends for help, he tries to commit suicide in order to cash in his life insurance.

Third Plot Point: Kingdom in Chaos

The Queen's attempt to protect her children without really assuming responsibility for leading them plunges the Kingdom into chaos as the Invaders breach the borders.

> **For Example:** In *A League of Their Own*, when Dottie's husband returns wounded from the war, she decides to leave the team just before the World Series and go home. She does this in part to force her younger sister Kit to get out from under her own shadow, but does it in a way that Kit interprets and resents as Dottie still "mothering" her.

Climax: Releases Her Children, Accepts Her Crown

The Queen accepts she must trust her children to embark on their own journeys and to play their own parts in protecting the Kingdom under her guidance. She knowingly and willingly leaves behind the Domestic World forever and takes her place as a true leader of the Kingdom.

> **For Example:** In *42*, Jackie Robinson leads the Brooklyn Dodgers into the final game "as a team."

Climactic Moment: Kingdom Is Saved

Working together, the Queen and her subjects are able to push back the Invaders and once again secure the borders of their Kingdom.

> **For Example:** In *The Post*, newspaper publisher Kay takes control of her "Kingdom" by daring to publish the revelation of a monumental government cover-up.

Resolution: Kingdom Prospers

The King is dead; long live the King. Having completed her arc, the Queen now ascends to the throne. No longer a Parent, she is now a Ruler. But her children are no longer Children (in the archetypal sense); they too have grown up. The cycle of life continues, and under her wise rulership, the Kingdom prospers.

> **For Example:** In *Return of the King*, Aragorn finally takes his throne as King of Gondor, restoring goodness to the realm as he begins his rule.

EXAMPLES OF THE QUEEN ARC

Examples of the Queen Arc include the following.

- Elizabeth I in *Elizabeth*
- Edna Spaulding in *Places in the Heart*
- George Bailey in *It's a Wonderful Life*
- Joan in *Joan of Arc*
- Harry Potter in *The Order of the Phoenix* (among other entries in the series)
- Aragorn in *The Lord of the Rings*
- Jackie Robinson in *42*

- Maximus in *Gladiator*
- Dottie Hinson in *A League of Their Own*
- Kay Graham in *The Post*
- Bob and Helen Parr in *The Incredibles*
- Arthur Pendragon in *King Arthur: Legend of the Sword*
- Wanda Maximoff in *WandaVision*
- Matthew Garth in *Red River*

"It is a glorious thing to stablish peace,
And kings approach the nearest unto God
By giving life and safety unto men."
—William Shakespeare

5
THE KING ARC

WHEN WE VIEW the human life and thus the six archetypal character arcs as taking on the classic story-structure format of Three Acts, it is no coincidence the all-important Midpoint marks the transition from the Queen Arc to the King Arc.

In any story, the structural Midpoint represents the turning point of the entire story. Within the plot, it signifies a shift out of the "reactive" phase, in which the protagonist has been distracted by the thematic Lie and by surface conflicts. Equally, it signifies the shift into the "active" phase, in which the protagonist begins to recognize what the conflict is really about and what antagonist he is really confronting. Thematically, this is represented by a Moment of Truth, in which the protagonist grasps the central Truth of his story (while not yet fully releasing or overcoming his personal Lie).

In our examination of the six life arcs, the middle two arcs of the cycle, comprising the "Second Act," are the Queen and the King. As discussed in the previous chapter, the Queen Arc ends with the protagonist having *become* a Ruler. Although not necessarily glimpsed within the Queen Arc itself, this signifies a total shift within the overall archetypal story. Up to this point, the arcs have represented the first half of life's concerns with the exterior world—with one's relationship to self, others, love, and power (from both positions of subordination and of authority).

Quite obviously, anyone inhabiting the King archetype has now reached the apex of temporal life. From here, it would seem there is nowhere to go but down, and in some ways this is true. From this point, the character descends (a symbolically important word) into the second half of life—into eventual old age, crippling mortality, and death. From here, temporal power wanes. Whether the character will rise to the even greater, and in some ways more powerful, challenges of the Third Act of life depends on his ability to successfully fulfill his final charge as King.

The King Arc, then, is about a character at the height of temporal power who is faced with the realization that the greatest good he can do for his beloved Kingdom—which he has so far proven himself so worthy to rule—is to sacrifice himself and surrender the throne. His arc quite literally ends with the traditional low moment of the Third Plot Point as the transition from life's Second Act to the Third Act.

The King Arc: Becoming the Sacrifice

The completion of the Queen Arc signified the rise of a worthy and aligned Ruler. Now represented as the King, this character is one who wields even greater power. Symbolically, he is the sovereign of a vast and successful empire. He is a good leader, possessing both the maturity to manage the Kingdom (in opposition to his passive counter-archetype the Puppet) and a true compassion for and understanding of his people (in opposition to the aggressive counter-archetype of the Tyrant—which we will discuss along with the Puppet in Chapter 12).

Now, times are changing. Not only does the King grow older, creating the need for him to prepare a worthy successor, but the Kingdom itself is about to face threats heretofore unheard of. Up to this point in his life, the King has proven his ability to courageously and successfully face down all manner of temporal antagonists. This time, however, the threat proves to be not of this world. A great and mysterious Cataclysm descends—and as the King will soon learn, this is a threat that cannot be fully defeated by the might of his arm. It can only be quenched if he is willing to surrender his power and sacrifice himself as propitiation.

Stakes: Glimpsing the Beginning of the End

When a character has everything, it is always clear he has everything to lose. For the King, the stakes are no longer about whether or not he will gain what he must in order to move forward in life. Rather, for the first time, the stakes are about whether or not he can understand he has reached the beginning of the end of his life and certainly his own temporal power. Can he let go and make the transition gracefully? Or will he hold on, in all futility, and devolve into the Tyrant?

Although the plot in a King Arc can be absolutely epic, it is a fundamentally spiritual arc—more so than any that have preceded it. The protagonist is now encountering life's *second* great threshold, or Door of No Return, which parallels the Hero's First Plot Point threshold. For the King, this threshold is truly crossed at his own story's Third Plot Point when he exits his temporal realm of power and begins his descent into what will become the spiritual realm of the Crone.

Antagonist: Confronting the Monsters at the Door

Similarly to how the Hero had to fight a Dragon to protect those he loved, the King must now sacrifice himself to the Cataclysm to safeguard the Kingdom. Just like old Beowulf the King, at the end of his saga, the King archetype offers himself to preserve and safeguard the Kingdom.

Although the Cataclysm may be initiated by other characters representing negative archetypes (such as the Tyrant, Witch, or Sorcerer), the Cataclysm itself isn't necessarily evil in nature. Rather, as a morally neutral force that must be appeased, it specifically represents the demands of Life and Death. The King cannot retain his power forever; to do so goes against all natural laws. If he is to continue his life's journey in grace and alignment—for the good of all—he must accept that.

Symbolically, the King surrenders into his Third Act as a ritual sacrifice of sorts. This demand for his "death" may look evil and horrible to the younger eyes of the Maidens, Heroes, and Queens. It may even seem so to the King himself to some extent since he does not yet understand the truths of life's Third Act. However, as with all the archetypal journeys, what this represents is simply the natural progression of all things.

The King surrenders himself to Death expecting nothing less, but he will be surprised (although not necessarily elated) to discover that this is not the end. Just as the Third Plot Point in story structure always symbolizes Death, it also always symbolizes (or at least offers the potential for) Rebirth. And so the King will come to glimpse the truth of life's Third Act, which can be spoken of in J.K. Rowling's beautiful line from *Harry Potter and the Deathly Hallows*:

> And then he greeted Death as an old friend, and went with him gladly, and, equals, they departed this life.

In short, the King will end by discovering that this great enemy he has been facing in the form of the Cataclysm has, all along, been his teacher.

(See Chapter 26 for a full exploration of the King's archetypal antagonists.)

Theme: Sacrificing a King for a Kingdom

At the Moment of Truth in his arc, the King will come to realize that the temporal battle on which his Maidens, Heroes, and Queens are focused is in fact not the victory the Kingdom needs. Thanks to this realization—and thanks ultimately to his true heart in understanding that a leader is really a servant to his people—he reveals himself as a worthy propitiation against this supernatural threat.

In essence, regardless of any opposing human characters, the true antagonist in the King Arc is a supernatural phenomenon—an unbalanced force that must be appeased. In *The Hero With a Thousand Faces*, Campbell references ancient traditions regarding the ritual "death of a king," which just as importantly speaks to the necessity of Old Age passing the torch of leadership on to the New Young.

KEY POINTS OF THE KING ARC

King's Story: An Awakening

King Arc: Leader to Elder (moves from Regal World to Preternatural World)

King's Symbolic Setting: Empire

King's Lie vs. Truth: Strength vs. Surrender

"Physical strength is the pinnacle of human achievement." versus "Spiritual strength requires me to relinquish my physical strength."

King's Archetypal Antagonists: Cataclysm and Rebel (see Chapter 26)

King's Relationship to Own Negative Shadow Archetypes:

Puppet finally wields his Power out of a growing Perception.

Tyrant learns to submit his Power to the bigger picture of Perception. (See Chapter 12)

King's Relationship to Subsequent Shadow Archetypes as Represented by Other Characters: Potentially rallies Hermit or defeats Witch with his sacrifice. (See Chapter 13)

THE BEATS OF THE KING ARC

1ST ACT: Regal World

Beginning: Replete But Vaguely Unsatisfied

The King has spent his reign fruitfully and faithfully, building the Kingdom into a powerful Empire. He is proud of how he cares for his people, knowing he has brought peace and prosperity through his wise reign. But even as he has grown complacent with his own power and wisdom, he has begun to sense in the rising twilight of his years that something is about to change within him—that it *must* change, that he cannot continue forever in the pleasing purpose of his power.

The world around him has grown up as well. His children/subjects are blooming into maturity, looking trustingly to him for guidance but also beginning to chafe against authority in their growing need for their own personal autonomy. It is a time of peak ripeness in the Kingdom—everything is good, but it also feels like the calm before the storm.

> **For Example:** In the beginning of *Black Panther*, de facto King T'Challa returns to his blessed and peaceful kingdom of Wakanda.

Inciting Event: Plea for Action Against Unprecedented Cataclysm

News arrives of a great Cataclysm impending upon the borders of the Kingdom. The Cataclysm is unprecedented and seems unstoppable, but the King and his subjects have faith: he has never yet faced something bigger than he could handle.

One of the messengers (or perhaps a Mage acting as the King's adviser) may insist this is totally different: it is a supernatural event. This sobers the King, but he doesn't take it too seriously. He refuses to respond to the Cataclysm as such and decides to treat it as he would any of the physical threats he has overcome so far during his reign.

> **For Example:** In *Casablanca*, expatriate Rick's little kingdom is increasingly threatened by news of World War II's encroachment.

2ND ACT: Preternatural World

First Plot Point: Confronts Cataclysm With Administrative and Military Might

As the Cataclysm draws nearer to the heart of the kingdom, the King rides out to face it for the first time. It is not what he expected: it *is* of another world. But it is not yet world-ending.

WRITING ARCHETYPAL CHARACTER ARCS | 89

He attacks the Cataclysm with his normal methods of administrative and military might, seeming to push it back, but in fact entangling it further with his Kingdom.

He also experiences the true threat of its power. Its eye is upon him, and it marks him in some dark way (perhaps in a physically destructive way, but certainly in a way that shifts his perspective of his "completeness" as King up to this point: he is a very small being in the face of this thing). He begins to comprehend his mortality.

> **For Example:** Although within the complex morality presented in Studio Ghibli's *Princess Mononoke*, Lady Eboshi is often thought of as the antagonist, she still represents a caring King archetype in her leadership of Iron Town. She does not know that in wounding the giant Boar, she is unleashing something supernatural.

First Pinch Point: Sword Breaks: The Old Methods of Success Aren't Working

After a series of seeming triumphs in which the King's choices nominally work in protecting the people from the Cataclysm, everyone is shocked and sobered when the King attempts a gambit against the Cataclysm only to lose his greatest symbol of power (his "sword"). His human might proves truly fallible against this inexplicable threat. Doubt of his ability to protect them (and rule them) begins to creep into his subjects' minds. Doubt begins to creep into his as well.

> **For Example:** In *The Avengers: Infinity War*, Tony Stark watches helplessly as everyone around him turns to dust when antagonist Thanos snaps his fingers and eliminates half the population of the universe.

Midpoint: Witnesses True Supernatural Nature of Cataclysm

The King confronts the Cataclysm with a full show of his kingly might—and is stunned in the midst of it all to realize his courage and his power mean nothing in the face of this unearthly force. He experiences a profound Moment of Truth, in which he realizes the Cataclysm cannot be faced, much less overcome, as he has overcome all other enemies: with mortal might. It is a supernatural force, and it will require a supernatural propitiation.

Most of his subjects do not see this. All they see is that their King has proven himself impotent against the storm. The entire Kingdom is shaken, as their King seems to withdraw from before this grave threat—not only impotent against it, but seemingly overcome by it.

> **For Example:** In *Harry Potter and the Deathly Hallows*, Harry's realization that Voldemort is pursuing the all-powerful Elder Wand signifies that Harry is not just opposing Voldemort but, in essence, Death itself.

Second Pinch Point: Rebellion: Subjects Lose Faith

The King—probably with the help of a Mage/Mentor character—begins to understand that the only way to stop the Cataclysm is to surrender his crown (and perhaps his life). His time as an earthly ruler is finished; it is time for him to give up his might, give up his youth, give up his strength, give up even his pride. He must begin the descent into the Underworld, humbling himself and accepting old age and death. He takes a few steps in this direction, beginning to shed his royal vestments in his preoccupation with understanding this supernatural antagonist.

His subjects witness this with increasing concern. They begin to lose faith in him as the King. The more unfaithful and aggressive among them (Rebels) push back with a semi-successful coup. The King and his plans are ultimately protected only by those who do remain faithful: the Heroes and Queens who also find themselves growing in maturity through this trial. Whether the King is captured or whether he goes into hiding, he is now separated from the majority of his kingly resources.

> **For Example:** In *Logan*, after barely escaping his own clone at the Munson Farm, Logan's increasing inability to heal his own wounds becomes obvious.

3RD ACT

False Victory: Tries to Stop the Cataclysm With Kingly Might

In response to the pleas of his followers and the demands of the Rebels, the King caves to his own deep desire to avoid sacrificing himself. He seizes a slight chance to stop the Cataclysm through physical means. He meets it "in the field" to do battle. He succeeds in some small measure, but the Cataclysm is not satisfied.

> **For Example:** In *Black Panther*, T'Challa accepts his half-brother Erik's challenge to fight for the throne, willing to sacrifice his body to the mortal antagonist but not yet ready to face the true Cataclysm of the deeper spiritual truth about what brought Erik to Wakanda.

Third Plot Point: Kingdom on the Brink

The Kingdom is now in true peril. The King's might could not stop the Cataclysm. His subjects reveal their true colors, some proving to be scoundrels, others proving their worth as his true successors. He is heartbroken by his subjects' suffering, even as he is agonized by the unavoidable necessity of his own sacrifice. Even as his loyal subjects suggest ways to try again in combating the Cataclysm, the King realizes what he must do.

> **For Example:** In *Braveheart*, William Wallace is betrayed by Robert the Bruce at the Battle of Falkirk, leading to his defeat and capture.

Climax: Bequeaths the Crown, Offers Self as Propitiation

The King passes his crown to his successor. At first, his subjects don't understand that he intends to offer himself as propitiation to the Cataclysm. When they do realize his intentions, they are horrified; they do not understand the supernatural aspect of the Cataclysm and do not understand how his sacrifice can help them. They try to stop him, but he will not be deterred.

> **For Example:** In *Casablanca*, recognizing the larger import of World War II, Rick sacrifices himself by sending his love Ilsa away with her freedom-fighter husband, while he himself enters the fray.

Climactic Moment: Sacrifices to Ensure Kingdom's Survival

The King, divested of his royalty, surrenders to the Cataclysm as a mere mortal—an old man who is willing to face death. His sacrifice is accepted, and the Cataclysm ends.

> **For Example:** In *Avengers: Endgame*, Tony accepts the final burden of defeating Thanos (a Greek word which, not so coincidentally, means "Death"). He snaps his fingers while wearing the Infinity Gauntlet, knowing it will mean his own end, as well as Thanos's.

Resolution: Departs Liberated Kingdom

The King departs the Kingdom, no longer as the King but as an Elder. He may literally die, or he may simply take on the Elder identity and leave the Kingdom to his successors. The Kingdom is at peace, free of the Cataclysm and prepared to begin a new era of prosperity under a new King trained by the old one.

> **For Example:** In *Dead Poets Society*, after unorthodox teacher John Keating is fired, he leaves the school, sadly, but knowing he has transformed the lives of his students.

EXAMPLES OF THE KING ARC

Examples of the King Arc include the following.

- Tony Stark in *Avengers: Infinity War* and *Avengers: Endgame*
- Lady Eboshi in *Princess Mononoke*
- Beowulf in *Beowulf*
- Rick Blaine in *Casablanca*
- Margaret Thatcher in *Iron Lady* (which sketches just about all the life archetypes, from Hero to Crone)

- T'Challa in *Black Panther*
- William Wallace in *Braveheart*
- Harry Potter in *The Deathly Hallows*
- John Keating in *Dead Poets Society*
- Marshall Pentecost in *Pacific Rim*
- Logan in *Logan*
- Aslan in *The Lion, the Witch, and the Wardrobe*
- King Theoden in *The Return of the King*
- Dalinar Kholin in The Stormlight Archives series
- Oedipus in *Oedipus Rex*

"...this land of death is dark and frightening.
No matter how deep the faith,
we each have to walk the lonesome valley;
we each have to walk it all alone.
[I]f we draw back from it
(and we are free to do so),
Kafka reminds us that 'it may be that
this very holding back is the one evil
you could have avoided.'"
—Madeleine L'Engle

6

THE CRONE ARC

WITHIN THE SAGA of the six archetypal character arcs, the two "elder" arcs that comprise the Third Act of life are perhaps the least dramatized. These arcs are those of the Crone and the Mage.

In studying these arcs and their analogous alignment to story structure, it becomes evident that the Third Act is, in itself, rather more mysterious than we give it credit for. In our modern storytelling, the Climax is meant not only to be the *point*, but also the most exciting moment in the story. And yet many views of story structure (not least the classic Hero's Journey) instead emphasize the Midpoint as the most significant moment in the plot, with the Third Act representing more of a resolution or summation.

It is interesting to acknowledge the parallels in this view of structure with that of human life itself. In many ways, a person's Third Act is the "quietest" time of life. What happens within it is notably influenced by the choices that have come before in the previous two acts. Now we have only to see how everything pans out.

But in many ways, this is only a surface view of the final act of life. If the Elders are no longer so embroiled in the challenges of survival and power that mark the earlier acts, they are no less involved in the final and in many ways the greatest challenge—the conundrum of a life that must end in death.

In our deeply death-averse culture, we have often avoided stories about the Third Act of life. This is both cause and effect to the reality that just as our modern societies lack crucial initiations for the young (as found in the Maiden and Hero Arcs), they also suffer from a dearth of true Elders—those who have legitimately completed all previous life arcs and are able to not only undertake their own final and most crucial arcs, but also to act as the archetypal Elders and Mentors who are so catalytic in impacting the younger arcs.

In short, I believe these arcs are desperately important and underserved. It is, in fact, difficult to think of many suitable story examples. Most of the time when a Crone or a Mage shows up in a story (especially a popular or genre story), he or she appears as a supporting character within the arc of a younger protagonist.

The Crone Arc begins the final act of these life arcs by presenting an inevitable and imperative Underworld Journey. Just as the transition from Queen to King marked the Midpoint or Moment of Truth in the overarching saga, the transition from King to Crone signifies the Third Plot Point. If you have studied story structure with me before, you already know the Third Plot Point is the doorway of Death and Rebirth.

The Crone Arc: Facing Down Death

The word "Crone" is a tricky one in some ways. This seems appropriate to me because the Crone herself is a tricky one. The word conjures images of a hook-nosed hag with a hairy wart on her lip. Gone is all the beauty of youth, to the point that her countenance is almost frightening. She lives alone, deep in the woods, discouraging contact with the curious and half-terrified children who seek her out to see if she is really the witch of local legend.

A popular figure in folk and fairy tales, she is often amoral, sometimes wreaking havoc on unwary villagers who dare trespass in her woods, sometimes offering surprising understanding and blessing—and usually the difference is decided by the worthiness of the intruder.

When we hear of the Crone, our response is often visceral and uncertain. But I have come to love the word, because the true Crone (and not her negative counter-archetypes of Hermit or Wicked Witch) is a portal to the deep wisdom of Elderhood. Her external beauty is vanished. Any temporal power or glory she won when she embodied the previous King archetype is long since abandoned. She gave it all, perhaps graciously but certainly not without heartbreak, in order to secure the Kingdom for her successors and journey on into the twilight.

In so many ways, the Crone archetype starts out broken. She who was once King is now fallen from all her power. No longer does she sit on a throne in the palace, but rather on a stool in a hut. No longer is she mighty, both physically and politically. Now, she is withered and weathered, hunched with rheumatism.

She can seem like a bit of a crank at first, but really this is because the great leap from the Second Act of her life to the Third is a lot to process. She has retreated to her hut in the woods in order to integrate, to process, to lick her wounds, and to grieve. As all Third Plot Points do, hers has demanded the complete death of the person she was. Her challenge, then, is to decide whether she will now accept the call to be rebirthed. She doesn't fully understand it yet, but in losing everything, she has in fact grown into something much greater.

At the beginning of her arc, the Crone is an Elder already—old and wise and possessing some magic. But, for all that, she is not greatly powerful. She is resigned to Death but still afraid of it. She knows her uses but doesn't find tremendous significance in her life. Whether gracefully or not, she is just waiting to die.

Therefore, hers is an arc from disempowerment to empowerment. Her "magic" evolves from little tricks (e.g., Gandalf the Grey's fireworks) to great strength (e.g., Gandalf the White's tremendous power).

Stakes: Literally Life and Death

The above is not to say the Crone has forsaken the Kingdom entirely. Her call to emerge once more from her solitude of contemplation and self-healing is likely to arrive in the form of a young Maiden or Hero who needs her help.

This younger character will come to her as a messenger of sorts, summoning her from her solitude with a challenge to confront the greatest enemy yet—a malignant evil—a superfluity of Death threatening the Kingdom. She accepts the call, thinking to herself, *I'm old, so, oh well, if I die, I die.*

But the journey becomes much more. It becomes a soul-deep sacrifice to protect the realm of Life. In the end, she chooses Life, not just her own or anyone's in particular, but Life itself—even though that will also mean accepting Death in all its profundity.

The King represented the sacrifice unto Death—the propitiating sacrifice to save the Kingdom. The Crone represents a resurrection—the symbolic return of Life.

Antagonist: Paying a Penny to the Ferryman

The adversary the Crone faces is Death made manifest. Within the plot, this antagonist may be externally represented as a Death Blight upon the Kingdom. This is not "natural" Death, but Death run rampant. This is Death that is out of balance with Life and overpowering it. More literally, this symbolism is merely representative of the human being's need to reconcile with her own mortality.

The Crone story may be as fantastic as that of Gandalf's descent into Khazad-dûm or as realistic as the quiet struggle with inexorable old age in Robert Redford and Jane Fonda's *Our Souls at Night*. It can be seen in the quiet isolation of characters such as Marilla Cuthbert at the beginning of *Anne of Green Gables*. There is even a bit of the Crone in Taika Waititi's wild tale of the orphan boy and his extremely cranky and unwilling foster father in his film *Hunt for the Wilderpeople*.

Whether symbolically or realistically, the Crone's journey is a descent into the Underworld. She pays her penny to the ferryman, crosses the River Styx, and goes to give Death a good talking to—while hopefully keeping her headstrong young charge from doing anything too stupid.

It's a tale that has fully as much scope for hilarity as for heaviness. But it is fundamentally a heavy theme—a confrontation with the final antagonist against whom all humans instinctively struggle and, if the arc completes, a recognition that Death may not have been what we always believed.

In *The Virgin's Promise*, Kim Hudson speaks of the Maiden's Third Plot Point beat as "Wandering in the Wilderness." I love this term not just for the Maiden but as an emotionally resonant description of all Third Plot Point experiences, including the entirety of the Crone Arc.

(See Chapter 27 for a full exploration of the Crone's archetypal antagonists.)

Theme: Choosing Descent and Return

The Crone's journey is perhaps the most terrifying of all the arcs. Correspondingly, the nadir of her descent offers the opportunity for the greatest riches of all.

In the end, the Crone's true transformation is not the decision to die as it was for the King. Rather, her crucial decision is to live again—to rise up and leave the Underworld rather than accept the temptation of old age's slow, resigned, comfortable descent into nothingness. In so rising, she symbolically raises the entire Kingdom with her—if not directly then at least by revealing the possibility and the way. She goes to Death seeking an enemy, but in the end she is surprised to find, if not a friend, then at least *not* an enemy.

The Crone's Moment of Truth at her Midpoint brings the revelation that she can "seek ye this day Life and not Death." But not until the end of her story, when she fully rejects the Lie that Death is something to be defeated rather than embraced, will she comprehend that indeed Death *is* Life—and become the Mage.

Key Points of the Crone Arc

Crone's Story: A Pilgrimage

Crone Arc: Elder to Sage (Uncanny World to Underworld)

Crone's Symbolic Setting: Underworld

Crone's Lie vs. Truth: Death vs. Life

"All life ends in death." versus "Life is Death and Death is Life."

Crone's Archetypal Antagonists: Death Blight and Tempter (see Chapter 27)

Crone's Relationship to Own Negative Shadow Archetypes:

Hermit finally accepts her Perception in order to grow into Wisdom.

Witch learns to submit her Perception to the truths of greater Wisdom. (See Chapter 13)

Crone's Relationship to Subsequent Shadow Archetypes as Represented by Other Characters: Potentially invigorates Miser or destroys Sorcerer through her wisdom. (See Chapter 14)

THE BEATS OF THE CRONE ARC

As with all the archetypes, the Crone can manifest within anyone's life at any time, if on a smaller scale. For example, any time a younger person faces an existential emergency—such as a midlife crisis—that person is very likely undergoing a Crone "subplot" as part of one of his or her larger arcs (i.e., because the Crone represents the "larger" Third Plot Point of the entire life cycle, she is always present, in some capacity, at the specific Third Plot Point within any of the previous arcs—see Appendix 2 for more information on these parallels).

1ST ACT: Uncanny World

Beginning: Lure of Retirement

The Crone lives alone in a hut on the edge of the village. She has stepped down from public life and service. Those who were once her subjects may approach her for guidance as an Elder, but she does not particularly encourage it. She is grumpy, worn, and hobbled by old age.

However, in completing the previous King Arc and crossing the last threshold into her Third Act, she broadened her understanding of the world beyond that of the temporal and into an acceptance of a greater spiritual realm. She works within that realm, making remedies and tinctures for herself and for those who might dare to ask for her help.

She's not exactly misanthropic, but she is deeply introverted, processing her transformation from King to Crone, from youth and power to old age and numinousness. She's retired. She's not entirely happy about it, but she has accepted it as unavoidable.

That acceptance has nudged her into lethargy. Even as she mourns the end of her vibrant Second Act, she also feels like she's *earned* her retirement. She's old and tired; she's accomplished more in her life than she ever knew possible. Rather than properly mourn her mortality and transform, she is tempted to just lie down and give up until Death comes to take her.

> **For Example:** In the beginning of *Anne of Green Gables*, Marilla Cuthbert is a sullen, unhappy woman who doesn't even realize how she has cut herself off from life.

Inciting Event: The Dream of Death

The Crone dreams a premonition about an imbalance between the forces of Life and Death. Death is coming to blight the land—either *directly* through a pestilence or apocalyptic event or *indirectly* through some sort of death culture. The choice to live and be alive is about to become very challenging for the world.

The Kingdom may be experiencing its first hint of this coming Blight. Most of the world will not recognize it for what it is (some even championing its advent). They lack the spiritual insight of an Elder to discern its true malignant nature.

A Hero or King may come to the Crone seeking guidance. She is resistant to rejoining the struggles of the larger Kingdom, but gives them a hint of the truth about what's really going on, her heart heavy with her own fear of Death.

For Example: In *The Fellowship of the Ring*, Gandalf the Grey begins to suspect the true malignant nature of Bilbo's ring after Frodo inherits it.

2ND ACT: Underworld

First Plot Point: Boards the Ferry

The Crone is drawn out from the retirement of her hut, perhaps by her Hero apprentice, perhaps by the entreaty of the King, or perhaps by a sign in her dreams. Grumpily, she agrees to go investigate, even though she still thinks it's a waste of time. Who can defeat Death, after all? Certainly, not her in all her feebleness.

But whether she admits it or not, hope sparks in her heart. Maybe Death *can* be defeated. One way or another, she figures that, since she is old and about to die anyway, she might as well see about doing one more good turn for "the grandchildren." Indeed, her love (symbolic or actual) for the Hero might be what finally prompts her to go forth to the River Styx and wait for the ferryman. She leaves behind the Kingdom and enters the Underworld, where she intends to see what this is all about and to try whatever tricks she may to delay Death.

> **For Example:** In Studio Ghibli's *Howl's Moving Castle* (which is a brilliant Crone-Arc-within-a-Maiden-Arc), Grandma Sophie treks into the Waste to try to regain her youth, enters the castle of the seemingly fearsome wizard Howl, and ends up involved in freeing the Kingdom from a malignant war.

First Pinch Point: Death Is Not Fooled by Her Little Tricks

In the Underworld, the Crone hobbles along, presenting (and mostly believing) herself as a harmless, helpless old woman. She proves canny. Her small magic tricks, such as they are, help her past her various obstacles on her way to discovering the source of the Death Blight.

WRITING ARCHETYPAL CHARACTER ARCS | 105

However, Death is not fooled, and neither is the Tempter (if there is a human antagonist causing the Blight—see Chapter 27). Emboldened by her success thus far, she tries one trick too many and is thwarted by a discovery of her true weakness. She is startled, because the weakness proves not to be the physical weakness she has identified with, but rather one of insight and perception. To a certain degree, she becomes even more frightened, but she is also intrigued. Her understanding is broadening; she has glimpsed the true power that could yet be available to her.

> **For Example:** In *The Hunt for the Wilderpeople*, antisocial widower Hec learns he is wanted by the authorities for "kidnapping" his foster son and taking him into the wilderness—even though the foster son was the one who doggedly followed Hec against Hec's adamant wishes.

Midpoint: Chooses to Seek Life

As the Death Blight descends upon the Kingdom, the Crone must make a choice: will she give up and return to her hut (or simply allow herself to be overtaken by nullity)? Or will she find the strength, courage, and liveliness to rise again, but in a new capacity—not a King and not a Crone, but the beginnings of a Mage?

She chooses Life, even though at this point that means fully facing her fear of Death. She chooses to rise up and stand against the Blight. She uses all her wily tricks to resist it. The Tempter is startled, both that she dares to present herself as an antagonist and also that she has the power to make any kind of dent against him. He does not yet take her as a serious threat, but for the first time, he does fully notice her as a spiritual power in her own right. He mostly wins the battle, but thanks to her choice, he is at least forced to pull back for a moment to reconsider his next move.

> **For Example:** In *Secondhand Lions*, Hub proves that "old age and treachery will always beat youth and exuberance" when he handily defeats a group of young bullies.

Second Pinch Point: Temptation

The Crone may guide the Hero, the Queen, and the King in erecting defenses. But she stands apart from the true struggle, working her magic behind the scenes, discovering her true Life power. She is confronted with a temptation. Now that she has chosen Life over Death, she becomes even more determined to live and not die.

The Tempter offers that she might become immortal: Death will never touch her. She intuits there is a great danger to this supposed gift, even though she does not yet fully grasp the truth that Death is Life and Life is Death. She does, however, understand that Death is important. She understands that however it may frighten her, its sheer necessity means it cannot be a wholly malignant force. She also inherently mistrusts the Tempter, even as he promises she will gain such power from this choice that she can save the Kingdom and stop Death (essentially becoming a Sorcerer).

She doesn't partake of the Tempter's gift and sends away the messenger, but she does keep the gift in her pocket—undecided about her proper course.

> **For Example:** In *Iron Lady*, an elderly Margaret Thatcher (suffering from dementia) is taunted by the "ghost" of her dead husband, but she refuses to "let him go."

3ᴿᴰ ACT

False Victory: Seeks Physical Immortality

The Kingdom is forced to a dire point. The young people about whom the Crone cares (particularly the Hero) are threatened, perhaps as a result of their own mistakes. She becomes very angry—both because of the suffering caused by the Death Blight and its threats, but also at the young people—their stupidity and their clear inability to be trusted with the Life of the Kingdom. She knows it is time to fully seek her power, but she does so by succumbing to the temptation of physical immortality. She doesn't complete the process, but her choice is enough to unleash the darkness.

> **For Example:** In *Up*, Carl's house (symbolizing his dead wife) is set on fire, and he has a meltdown in which he alienates and endangers his young companion Russell.

Third Plot Point: Death Prevails

Empowered, the Tempter looses the Death Blight upon the Kingdom. The Angel of Death descends; Life begins not to be blotted out as the Crone feared, but to be overtaken by Death: zombified. The lines between Life and Death blur, and the horror is greater than if Death itself had prevailed. The Crone is aghast at her choice, recognizing that she was the one who skewed the balance of light and dark, Life and Death.

> **For Example:** In *Anne of Green Gables*, Marilla realizes, on the eve of sending Anne back to the orphanage for stealing her brooch, that Anne was in fact innocent.

Climax: Embraces Death

The Crone is deeply humbled. She casts away the immortal power she has been offered. She recognizes Death not as an enemy but as the lover of Life. Life cannot exist without Death, just as the day cannot be without the night. She submits herself to the beautiful transformation of life. She does this with some hope of rectifying her mistakes, but largely she does it in total humility, simply awed and prostrate before the light of truth. She walks willingly through Death's door to meet her fate.

> **For Example:** In *Fellowship of the Ring*, Gandalf the Grey sacrifices himself to the Balrog ("You shall not pass!") in order to salvage the rest of the Fellowship.

Climactic Moment: Death Transformed

Her wisdom transforms her from the mortal and feeble Crone into a powerful Mage. Death, now that it has been seen as beautiful through her eyes, is itself transformed. She has the power to thwart the Tempter and to restore the balance of Life and Death, lifting the Blight from the Kingdom even though she still cannot banish Death itself.

For Example: In *Howl's Moving Castle*, Sophie (who has slowly regained her youth) rescues Howl from transforming himself into a monster.

Resolution: Reintegrates Into Renewed Kingdom

The Kingdom doesn't fully understand what happened. They only know the Crone emerged from the Underworld, not only resurrected but transformed. They are in awe of her and more than a little frightened. They recognize in her a great new power, which they both trust and fear. They are happy the Blight has lifted, even though they might be a little confused or even disgruntled that she did not end Death altogether. But she is wise and calm. She just smiles and does not tell them truths they are not ready to hear.

She is formally reintegrated into a respected role in the Kingdom, but even though she leaves her hut behind, it is not to return to the palace. Rather, she embarks on a mission that will take her all around the world as the Mage (which we will discuss in the next chapter).

For Example: At the end of *Iron Lady*, Margaret lets go of her hallucinations of her dead husband and surprises her daughter by "returning to the land of the living."

EXAMPLES OF THE CRONE ARC

Examples of the Crone Arc include the following.

- Sophie Hatter in *Howl's Moving Castle*
- Elderly Margaret Thatcher in *The Iron Lady*
- Gandalf the Gray in *The Fellowship of the Ring*
- Hub McCann in *Secondhand Lions*
- Hec in *The Hunt for the Wilderpeople*
- Louis Waters and Addie Moore in *Our Souls at Night*
- Henry Dailey in *The Black Stallion*
- Marilla and Matthew Cuthbert in *Anne of Green Gables*
- Hepzibah in *Lantern Hill*
- Carl Fredricksen in *Up*
- Ista in *Paladin of Souls*

- Ebenezer Scrooge in *A Christmas Carol*
- Master Shifu in *Kung-Fu Panda*
- Rooster Cogburn in *True Grit*
- Alan Grant in *Jurassic Park*

"The true value of a human being
can be found in the degree
to which he has attained liberation
from the self."
—Albert Einstein

7
THE MAGE ARC

THE FINAL TWO archetypal character arcs in the life cycle deal primarily with questions of Mortality—and thus inevitably with the ultimate questions about the meaning of life.

So far, we've viewed the six life arcs as part of a unified story structure of Three Acts. The First Act—featuring the Maiden and the Hero—focused on overcoming challenges of Fear in integrating the parts of oneself and individuating. The Second Act—the Queen and the King—focused on challenges of Power and on integration in relationship to others. Finally, the Third Act—the Crone and the Mage—turned its attention to Mortality and to the integration of soul and spirit.

As we discussed in the previous chapter, the Crone Arc represented the complete transition of the character from the "outer" world struggles with one's self and other people into the "inner" world struggles with more existential and spiritual crises. Although anyone who lives long enough will reach the Crone Arc at least chronologically, not everyone will accept her challenge and fulfill her difficult arc of embracing her own mortality. Therefore, even fewer among us will get the opportunity to truly take on the deep mysteries of the powerful Mage Arc.

In part because of that fact itself, the Mage Arc *is* mysterious. We see this most plainly through the metaphor of fantasy stories that offer up a supernatural Mentor to a world in need. Yet rarely is this character the protagonist. Even more rarely is the Mage fully embodied in a "realistic" story. When the Mage *does* show up in a real-world story, his deep, almost otherworldly wisdom inevitably brings with it a touch of the magical—as, for example, with Will Smith's wise and mysterious caddy in the golf movie *The Legend of Bagger Vance*.

This doesn't necessarily mean the character is literally magical in any way. But it does mean the character has not only glimpsed but assimilated truths about life that most people don't even know exist. By accepting his own mortality back in the Crone Arc, he has now reached a new level of transformation, objectivity, and wisdom.

For the Mage, who has already accepted Death, what is there now left to transform? What is left, of course, is the final threshold to cross in earnest. But there is also the final temptation. How will he use his great power and wisdom, the riches of his entire well-spent life? Will he use it to guide those he loves? Or to control them in ways to which he has no right? Will he surrender—or will he become a Sorcerer?

THE MAGE ARC: JOINING GOD

Although the Mage can be played by a younger character, the arc itself is representative of the final chapter of one's life. The Mage represents a person who has successively and positively completed all six life arcs. This is an unusual and extraordinary achievement. Merely reaching the end of our lives doesn't mean we'll go out as Mages. The Mage, then, is someone who put in an unfailing amount of work throughout his life, someone who consistently sought light and truth—and was rewarded in that search.

Now, he has almost reached the end. Not only has he all but reached the end of his mortal life due to his great age, but he has also reached nearly the end of the many challenges that weigh us down in our earlier acts by transcending his ego.

But however wise the Mage may be, he is still a body on this earth, and he has not yet surrendered *everything*. There remain things he cares about, causes in which he passionately believes. However burnt out the ego may be, there is still a flickering spark. He has the ability and the insight to not just guide those who are coming up behind him, but to shape and even control certain outcomes. How he uses his power and how ready he is to truly shed the things of this world and step willingly into Death will be the mark of his final successful arc.

Stakes: Leaving Behind a Good World for Those Who Follow

As with all good stories, life has a tendency to come full circle. Grandparents often become increasingly focused on the legacy they will leave to their beloved descendants. Physically, they sometimes even return to the very same hearth at which they themselves leaned on their own grandparents' knees, hearing stories of adventures long past.

It is no wonder we most often recognize the Mage in his Flat-Arc form of Mentor. The deeper we get into the life arcs, the more frequently we see previous archetypes showing up in some version of their own stories. And so the Mage Arc inevitably runs concurrently with the younger arcs, particularly those of Hero and King. The Mage is the wise voice in their ears, initiating them and guiding them to see what they do not yet have the maturity or the experience to see for themselves.

The Mage cares deeply about whether these younger characters will fulfill their arcs. Will they be able to face the same challenges he did? Will they overcome? How will they be able to resist the temptations of sloth and power that are present in their counter-archetypes if the Mage does not take care to protect them from themselves?

The Mage's challenge is very much represented in the anecdote about the boy who waited and waited for his caterpillar to emerge from its cocoon. When the time came and he witnessed how terribly the butterfly struggled to free itself, he "helped" by clipping open the cocoon. He did not realize the butterfly's struggle out of the tight cocoon was what forced the blood into its beautiful wings. This butterfly emerged with its wings impossibly swollen and limp—and, to the boy's chagrin, it died.

The Mage, who holds so much power to shape the lives of those he loves, faces the primary challenge of letting them go. He must let them face their own struggles and make their own mistakes. Not only is this crucial to the continuance of healthy life-arc cycles after him, it is also his final challenge in shedding his remaining burdens of this world so that he may step freely into the next.

Antagonist: Understanding the Nature of Evil

The external conflict in a Mage story may be represented by relatively mundane threats. This is because what now threatens the physical Kingdom is necessarily a threat "of this world" and rightly pertaining, in fact, to the conflicts of earlier arcs. The Kingdom is under dire threat—perhaps by the Hero's Dragon, the Queen's Invaders, or the King's Cataclysm—but *that* threat will ultimately be faced by the younger archetypes.

It is true the Mage is there to help them understand their duties, but more than that, he is there to combat an even more archetypal antagonist the others cannot yet see—Evil itself. This can be recognized in the beautiful fantasy stories of *The Lord of the Rings* and *Harry Potter*, both of which feature Mentor/Mage characters—Gandalf the White and Dumbledore, respectively—who guide the younger archetypes in taking on more corporeal antagonists while the Mages themselves use their power against a much greater Evil.

(See Chapter 28 for a full exploration of these archetypal antagonists.)

Theme: Journeying On

However epic the stakes may (or may not) be in the story's external conflict, the Mage's story is ultimately one of tying off loose ends and ending the tale. It is about ending one's life well and dying a good death.

The Mage need not literally die in your story (especially if he is represented by a younger character). But he will almost certainly journey on in some respect, even if it is just walking off into the sunset like Bagger Vance or, in a more symbolic version, "diminishing into the West" like Galadriel after resisting the final temptation of the Ring's power.

If the Mage character does die, the death may either be a voluntary choice in some sense (such as Obi-Wan Kenobi's sacrificing himself to Darth Vader in *A New Hope* or Dumbledore's plot with Snape in *The Half-Blood Prince*) or at least a death to which he goes without regret or reluctance (as does Yoda in *Return of the Jedi* and Garth and Hub McCann in *Secondhand Lions*). He represents someone "who has fought the good fight and finished his race."

Key Points of the Mage Arc

Mage's Story: A Mission

Mage Arc: Sage to Saint (Liminal World to Yonder World)

Mage's Symbolic Setting: Cosmos

Mage's Lie vs. Truth: Attachment vs. Transcendence

> "My love must protect others from the difficult journey of life." versus "True love is transcendent and allows life to unfold."

Mage's Archetypal Antagonists: Evil and the Weakness of Humankind (see Chapter 28)

Mage's Relationship to Own Negative Shadow Archetypes:

Miser finally opens himself up through his Wisdom to gain Transcendence.

Sorcerer learns to surrender his worldly wisdom in exchange for true Transcendence. (See Chapter 14)

The Beats of the Mage Arc
1ST ACT: Liminal World
Beginning: Powerful But Limited

The Mage is an enlightened person—someone who has understood and accepted the vast and paradoxical partnership of Life and Death. He walks the Liminal World—an existence that is neither Life nor Death but between them. He has no particular home, but roves the land, moving from problem spot to problem spot, helping resolve magical hang-ups or solve disputes via his otherworldly wisdom.

He is greatly revered and loved, seen by some as an avuncular friend and by others as a fearsome mystical force. He loves others, but really he loves all—living in a calm neutrality that sees the greater purposes at work in Life's systems.

He is a friend of Death—but not of Evil, which he has learned to distinguish as not Death itself but the death urge or the addiction to power (being the power over Life and Death). As such, he is careful of his own power, recognizing himself not as a master but as a servant. In previously overcoming his fear of Death, he also largely transcended his ego.

> **For Example:** In *The Legend of Bagger Vance,* the mysterious caddy and golf expert shows up, seemingly out of nowhere and seemingly in need of a job from the one person who most needs his help.

Inciting Event: Revelation/Rise of Evil

At one of the stops along his pilgrimage, the Mage learns of "a disturbance in the Force." He learns Evil has returned or is lurking, awaiting the alignment of events. The Mage is deeply disturbed, not only because he stands opposed to Evil, but because he fears for the suffering and misguidance that may be inflicted on the Kingdom and its children, whom he loves.

He may here enlist a Hero to help him, either to hold the fort while he's gone or to accompany him on his mission to seek out the source of this threat of Evil and hopefully cut it off at the pass. But the Hero dawdles, and the Mage must start the action on his own.

> **For Example:** In *The Miracle on 34th Street*, when Kris Kringle realizes the true spirit of Christmas has been forgotten amidst all the commercialism and cynicism, he agrees to take a job as Santa Claus in Macy's Department Store.

2ND ACT: Yonder World

First Plot Point: Climbs the Mountain

The Mage climbs the mountain, bravely ascending to the Yonder World because only he has the power and insight to do so. He is allowed to understand the full threat of the Evil.

He may confront a Sorcerer who has been corrupted into a conduit for Evil, or he may witness Evil itself. He may wrestle with his own dilemma, fighting against the need to surrender and the idea that true love is transcendent.

The Hero may accompany him or may go off on his own quest. He is unlikely to ascend the mountain with the Mage, but if he does, he will not be able to see or comprehend the full extent of the supernatural that the Mage does.

> **For Example:** In *The Ten Commandments*, Moses ascends Mt. Sinai to receive the Ten Commandments from God. (He leaves his protégé Joshua halfway up the mountain.)

First Pinch Point: Evil Infiltrates the Camp of Man

The courage of man begins to fail. In the face of this great Evil, some waver in their goodness when confronted by their fear of Death. Compromises and deals with the devil are made. The Hero is abused for his efforts to aid the Mage and is also tempted from his path. The Mage returns to scold and advise the people of the Kingdom. Even in his profound wisdom, he is deeply invested in their fate. He doesn't want them to suffer or to choose the wrong path. He mentors them.

> **For Example:** In *To Kill a Mockingbird*, Atticus insists his son Jem spend a month reading to a crotchety old lady after Jem destroyed her flowers in a fit of rage.

Midpoint: Confronting Evil—and Also Evil in the Heart of Man

The Mage loves his world and his people. He wants to help them as a good Father/Grandfather should. But he is beginning to realize he cannot help them. They must help themselves. In a great battle or time of need, he may confront Evil itself to clear a path for them (to keep it a "fair fight"), but he cannot defeat the evil inclinations in their own hearts. He can only stand by and wait and hope.

But even his hope is a source of inner conflict. He is caught between the urge to save them and the need to access the surrendered love of detachment.

Thanks in part to the Mage's intervention (and also his counsel), the Kingdom escapes destruction although perhaps not defeat. The Hero rallies to his true identity and strength, in no small part because his love for the Mage causes him to want the Mage to be proud of him and pleased by his efforts.

> **For Example:** In *Mary Poppins*, Mary maneuvers the children's neglectful father into taking them with him to his job at the bank.

Second Pinch Point: Heart Is Broken by Man's Suffering

Man is betrayed by Man. The Hero is in bad straits, broken, doubting, suffering. The Mage is deeply wounded by his love for them all. He is challenged in his growing realization that true Love is transcendent and cannot make choices for others in order to protect them from their own mistakes. The Mage comforts the Hero and others but hasn't much else to offer. He rages within himself, struggling and angry that it should be so.

> **For Example:** In *Miracle on 34th Street*, Kris is incensed when he hears that his young ward who enjoys playing Santa Claus for the benefit of younger children has been told by the store psychiatrist that something is wrong with this desire.

3ʳᴰ ACT

False Victory: Refuses to Interfere With Man's Choices —and Man Chooses Wrong

The Mage wins his inner battle and makes the hard choice to let the Kingdom dwellers, including his Hero, go forth and make exactly the wrong choice. There is tremendous fallout, but the Mage must stand back, seemingly callous, and watch, trusting that it is part of a bigger plan, which he is now coming into alignment with.

> **For Example:** In *Doctor Strange*, the Ancient One allows herself to die.

Third Plot Point: Brink of Annihilation

The Kingdom faces death in the external conflict. The Mage, however, faces transformation—the choice to finally and fully step into the Yonder World (i.e., Death).

> **For Example:** In *The Return of the Jedi*, Yoda recognizes it is his time to return to the Force.

Climax: Meeting With the Divine

In the midst of his annihilation/transformation, the Mage is confronted by the Divine and is thus raised above the mortal world of men, including their limited insight and emotion. He will finish what he started as the Crone, this time literally leaving Death for Life.

> **For Example:** In *Fellowship of the Ring*, Galadriel passes her final test of refusing the One Ring's power, even though she knows it means she "will now diminish" and "pass into the West."

Climactic Moment: Evil Redeemed/Destroyed

The Mage does not directly interfere in the great battle against Evil, but the Hero and others see him and are inspired to pursue Good against Evil whatever the cost. He inspires them to seek hope. Through his inspiration and their efforts, Evil is either redeemed or destroyed.

> **For Example:** On the last hole, Bagger Vance steps back to let his student make his own decision about whether or not he will win the game by cheating.

Resolution: Kingdom Renewed for Another Cycle

The Mage says his goodbyes, engulfing the sorrow of his children in great love, as he prepares to journey on to the heavens.

> **For Example:** Mary Poppins leaves the Banks family, sad to go because she loves them but knowing it is best for them to make do on their own now.

EXAMPLES OF THE MAGE ARC

For reasons already mentioned, I found it difficult to discover many examples of a Mage Arc undertaken by a protagonist, so many of the following examples include characters who are more properly "Mentors" in someone else's story (we will discuss the Flat archetype of the Mentor in more detail in Chapter 21).

- Kris Kringle in *The Miracle on 34th Street*
- The Ancient One in *Doctor Strange*
- Yoda in *Star Wars*
- Alfred Pennyworth in *Batman*
- Galadriel in *The Lord of the Rings*
- Garth McCann in *Secondhand Lions*
- Atticus Finch in *To Kill a Mockingbird*
- The Oracle in *The Matrix*
- Mary Poppins in *Mary Poppins*
- Bagger Vance in *The Legend of Bagger Vance*
- Penelope Keeling in *The Shell Seekers*

Part 2:
The Twelve
Shadow Archetypes

"Whether creative possibilities
or regressive destruction shall prevail
depends not upon the nature
of the archetype or myth,
but upon the attitude and degree
of consciousness."
—Edward Whitman

8

INTRODUCTION TO THE TWELVE SHADOW ARCHETYPES

WHERE THERE IS light, there is shadow. Where there is a right way to do something, there are usually several ways to do it wrong. So it goes with archetypal character arcs and their potential shadow archetypes—of which there are *two* for every positive archetype.

Throughout the first section of this book, we have explored six successive life arcs, represented by the Positive Change Arcs of six primary archetypes—the Maiden, the Hero, the Queen, the King, the Crone, and the Mage. Each of these positive archetypes represents a rising above the limitations of the previous archetype in the cycle. But they also represent a struggle with related "shadow" or negative archetypes. Each positive archetype sits at the top of a triangle that is completed by a potential negative polarity between the two negative archetypes—one representing an aggressive shadow archetype and the other representing a passive shadow archetype.

This is why one of the primary challenges within any of the six positive archetypal arcs is that of grappling with the conflicting *desire for* and *fear of* autonomy. Only in integrating and accepting the responsibility for this growing power is a character able to escape the beckoning shadow archetypes and instead level up into the subsequent life arc.

Twelve Shadow or Negative Archetypes

More or less classically, the corresponding archetypes can be viewed like this:

1. **Positive:** Maiden
   Passive: Damsel
   Aggressive: Vixen

2. **Positive:** Hero
   Passive: Coward
   Aggressive: Bully

3. **Positive:** Queen
   Passive: Snow Queen
   Aggressive: Sorceress

4. **Positive:** King
   Passive: Puppet
   Aggressive: Tyrant

5. **Positive:** Crone
   Passive: Hermit
   Aggressive: Witch

6. **Positive:** Mage
   Passive: Miser
   Aggressive: Sorcerer

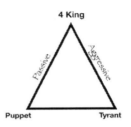

WRITING ARCHETYPAL CHARACTER ARCS | 131

Just as the temptation and struggle against the shadow archetypes' corruption is inherent within all of the archetypal Positive Change Arcs, so too are the two negative archetypes inherent within each other. Although a character representing a negative archetype will usually manifest most obviously as one or the other—passive or aggressive—they are really just two sides of the same coin. For example, inherent within any Coward is usually a latent Bully, just as the Bully is often a Coward at heart.

There are many ways negative archetypes can arc in a story:

- From negative to positive (a Positive Change Arc)
- From positive to negative (a Negative Corruption Arc)
- From passive to aggressive (a Negative Fall Arc)
- From aggressive to passive (which is not exclusive to but can be seen in a Negative Disillusionment Arc)
- Not at all (a negative Flat Arc, in which the character is less likely to be the protagonist and more likely to be the antagonist in someone else's Positive Change Arc or a negative Impact Character in someone else's Negative Change Arc)

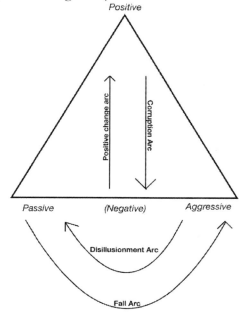

THE PASSIVE COUNTER-ARCHETYPES

The passive archetypes represent a fatal immaturity. No matter at what stage characters find themselves within the life arcs, their first challenge will be to resist their own sense of complacency and safety—which works to keep them where they are. Although they have little choice about whether or not they will be called into the journey of a subsequent archetype, they can decide whether they will grow or whether they will resist.

The passive shadow archetypes are the result of a refusal to grow into the next arc. They represent an attempt to maintain power in its *former* guise. For example, someone who has successfully completed the Hero Arc and is now being challenged to grow into the Queen Arc may resist the call of leadership and responsibility by hiding away within the selfish passivity of the Snow Queen. Life is demanding this character change, but the character resists, is unable to overcome fear, and fails to complete her proper growth. As a result, the character ends emotionally stunted and unfit to take on the responsibilities that life has now bestowed.

In short, facing the passive archetype is one of the earliest steps in any positive archetype's forward struggle. This fearful shadow aspect of one's self represents what we often hear spoken of within the Hero's Journey as the Hero's "Refusal of the Call to Adventure." Put simply: he's scared. And considering the immensity of the journey before him, we can all commiserate with exactly why that is.

When the Hero—or any other positive archetype—succumbs to this fearful part of himself, he aborts not just the journey but his own ability to grow and mature. In this instance, he will get stuck as the Coward, and his own progress forward in life will become immeasurably more difficult.

THE AGGRESSIVE COUNTER-ARCHETYPES

By contrast, the aggressive polarity of the negative archetypes represents not so much a fear of reality but a related desire to control it. Although the aggressive archetypes are literally the polar opposite of the passive archetypes, the passive archetypes are still often at the root of a character's aggression. In many ways, the aggressive archetypes represent an overcompensation in response to the character's inner fear of change and growth.

Even though the aggressive archetypes appear much more proactive and productive than do the passive archetypes, they too represent a stagnation. They may be "getting things done" within their realm of activity, but they are not actually moving forward.

For example, a Crone who has refused to take her journey into the Mage may get stuck in the aggressive polarity of the Witch—using the not-inconsiderable power she has gleaned throughout her long life to control others and manipulate outcomes. The Witch looks powerful, but unlike the Crone she is not expanding. She represents not just a stillness within the character's maturation, but a stagnation. She has gotten stuck through her own apathy and fear, has refused (however unconsciously) to continue growing, and has instead turned her energy outward upon a world she resents.

How the Shadow Archetypes Relate to the Thematic Truth/Lie

As we've already discussed, the six archetypal Positive Change Arcs represent the character's ability to transition away from a limiting life belief, a Lie, and into an acceptance of an archetypal Truth.

These same archetypal Lies/Truths are also inherent within the related negative shadow archetypes. The difference is that these negative archetypes resist the Truth. Through fear of change or desire for control, they cling to a broken version of reality. Depending on the type of Negative Change Arc they undergo (Disillusionment, Corruption, or Fall), they will encounter various opportunities to acknowledge and accept the Truth. In a true Negative Change Arc, they will fail to take advantage of these opportunities, and the metaphorical Kingdom will always suffer as a result.

How the Shadow Archetypes Relate to the Positive Arcs

Within all types of archetypal stories, we always have the opportunity for a full cast. Just as the negative polarities are present to some degree within the protagonist of a Positive Change Arc, so too can the positive archetype be glimpsed inside the protagonist of a Negative Change Arc.

More than that though, we have the opportunity to externalize these struggles into the supporting cast. As we've seen in earlier chapters, the Hero's Journey prominently features more advanced archetypal characters in supporting roles, most notably the King and the Mage/Mentor.

Likewise, negative archetypes frequently show up in villain roles. I haven't observed a hard-and-fast pattern, but it resonates that a powerful use of negative archetypes within a positive-archetype story is that of presenting the protagonist with a villain of the subsequent archetype (usually the aggressive polarity). For example, a Queen almost always has to confront and overcome a Tyrant, which is the aggressive counter-archetype for the subsequent arc of King.

Not only does this approach provide opportunities for a solid plot-theme connection, it also offers the always brilliant chance to symbolically represent the antagonist as a shadow version of the protagonist's potential self. As such, the antagonist can offer both temptation to the growing protagonist of the power she might wield, as well as a caution of what kind of monster she might turn into should she succumb to that temptation.

The same goes for the characters in a Negative Change Arc story. If the protagonist represents a negative archetype such as the Sorceress, the rest of the cast can be used to represent supporting archetypes that deepen the thematic and symbolic narrative.

As you can already see, there are many possible variations that may arise when a character falls away from the health of the positive archetypes and into the unhealth of the negative archetypes. Because there are *many* possible narratives for representing the negative archetypes in the protagonist of a Negative Change Arc, I won't be offering a "mythic beat sheet" for each of the negative archetypes in the same way I have done for the positive archetypes.

Over the course of the next six chapters, we will dive more deeply into the partnership of each passive/aggressive polarity and talk about how you can recreate these important archetypes within your own stories.

"One is bound in by the walls of childhood; the father and mother stand as threshold guardians, and the timorous soul, fearful of some punishment, fails to make the passage through the door and come to birth in the world without."
—Joseph Campbell

9

Damsel and Vixen

WITHIN THE JOURNEY of life's story, the first challenge is that of becoming an autonomous individual—an independent and responsible adult. However obvious that may be, the journey itself cannot be taken for granted. Indeed, although we may all grow up chronologically, the struggle to truly leave childhood behind is one that is often prolonged and even aborted for a great many.

Within the model of the six transformative character arcs, the first initiatory journey is represented by the archetype of the Maiden (whose journey we discussed in Chapter 2). She faces external antagonists who are metaphorically and often literally represented by the Too-Good Mother, the Naïve Father, and the Predator-Groom who would devour her youth and innocence. But she also faces *internal* danger from the shadowy counter-archetypes of fear and egoism that would prevent her from embracing a new perspective and completing her journey.

For the Maiden, these shadow archetypes are represented by the Damsel and the Vixen. The Damsel represents the passive polarity within the Maiden's shadow, the Vixen the aggressive polarity.

Before we dig into these important archetypes, I will address their titles, since both archetypes are fraught with controversy in modern portrayals.

The Damsel, of course, represents the much-discussed damsel in distress so often objectified within the Hero's Journey. Recognizing how the Damsel has often been reduced to a stereotype is important, but it is also important not to discredit the psychological reality of the archetype itself. For instance, even her role within the Hero Arc is actually not without cause, as we discussed in Chapter 3, since rescuing the Damsel—as played by any character—is an important symbolic moment within the Hero Arc. This is especially so because the Damsel should be seen to represent not just a separate individual character, but in fact a part of the Hero's own psyche (as is true of all characters within any particular journey).

An equally troublesome archetype/stereotype in today's media is what I have chosen to term the Vixen. Kim Hudson, author of *The Virgin's Promise*, and others use the name Whore for this archetype, but to me this seems a bit much for such a young archetype. The Whore *is* a viable archetype of its own, but because it has been used so often to stereotype female sexuality, it requires the same caution as for the Damsel.

In any examination of the Maiden's aggressive shadow archetype, whatever you wish to call it, it is important to recognize that the comparatively powerless Maiden has fewer resources at her disposal when in her aggressive shadow archetype than do any of the successive archetypes. Instead of controlling others as she would be able to do in the aggressive forms of later arcs (such as the King/Tyrant), she is only able to use what skills her childhood has so far given her. This often takes the form less of actual aggression with others and more of attempts at manipulation. Inevitably, this shadow archetype is one of the most tragic, since it represents a vulnerable character who is selling off far more of herself than she is able to get in return from others.

THE DAMSEL: A PASSIVE REFUSAL TO INITIATE INTO ADULTHOOD

Like all the passive archetypes, the Damsel carries a frozen shard of fear in her heart. As the youngest of the negative archetypes, her fear is largely unformed and unnamed. There is a deep innocence to it. She has depended on others all her life to take care of her, and (unlike the Vixen) she has probably been comparatively lucky in that there were people to do so.

But via her very innocent cared-for-ness, she has never been challenged to rise up. Even if the fear is implicit and unnamed, she is afraid of having to fend for herself. Not only has she never before had to take responsibility for herself, but she has also probably been discouraged from doing so.

Like Rapunzel in *Tangled*, the Damsel has been told "Mother Knows Best" and "kept safe" through fearsome stories of the wicked adult world. But as Zora Neale Hurston says so fiercely:

> If you are silent about your pain, they'll kill you and say you enjoyed it.

Most of the passive archetypes represent a sort of faux "goodness"—or at least an attempt on the character's part to avoid being bad. But this avoidance is not active; it is passive. Because it is rooted in fear, it ultimately leads the character to avoid the wrong choice by refusing to make any choice at all.

In the beginning, while still a Child, the Damsel's apparent goodness may seem like maturity. She may be praised for being too "wise" and "mature" to make the seemingly reckless mistakes of the Maiden—which she herself confuses with the unhealthy aggression of the Vixen. As time goes on, and life demands she grow up whether she's ready or not, her true lack of maturity begins to show through. She is not prepared to take care of herself; she lacks both the wisdom and the experience. Contrary to what she has always believed, there *will* come a day when no one rides in to save her. At the moment when she is truly confronted with the challenges of autonomy, she will discover that her supposed maturity leaves her defenseless.

THE DAMSEL'S POTENTIAL ARCS: POSITIVE AND NEGATIVE

Within most Maiden Arcs, the protagonist almost always starts out in a very Damsel-like space. This means that, dormant within the Damsel, is all the Maiden's potential. Even if she gets stuck in the Damsel space far beyond what would be chronologically preferable, she is like a seed in the winter ground. All the necessary energy for transformation and growth is still latent within her. Particularly since the Child marks the beginning of the entire cycle of life arcs, there resides within her great potential for a Positive Change Arc.

Equally, however, there is the potential for a Negative Change Arc. If she stays too long a Damsel, she may devolve into her aggressive polarity—the Vixen. But she may also simply regress deeper into a determinedly "innocent" and "helpless" state, refusing to face life head on and instead relying on Blanche DuBois's "kindness of strangers" to get through life. But as with Blanche in *A Streetcar Named Desire*, this determined refusal to grow only nudges her down the line of passive, stunted archetypes as she grows older.

THE VIXEN: A MANIPULATIVE/AGGRESSIVE ATTEMPT TO AVOID THE INITIATION INTO ADULTHOOD

Like all the aggressive polarities, the Vixen possesses at least a little more consciousness than the Damsel. She sees enough to recognize her antagonists, to resent restraint upon her existence, and to take advantage of what power is immediately available.

In contrast to the Damsel, her courage extends beyond what Clarissa Pinkola Estés terms "doing nothing out of fear of doing the wrong thing." But this is not to say that she, too, isn't terrified of growing up and claiming her true power—along with its responsibility. What courage she has is not enough to let her brave the soul-changing difficulties of a true Maiden Arc—which would end with her individuating from her Authority Figures. The result is that, despite whatever power she believes she wields through her rebellion and manipulation, she is just as helpless as the Damsel.

Just as the Damsel is often represented as the Good Girl, the

WRITING ARCHETYPAL CHARACTER ARCS | 143

Vixen is inevitably the Bad Girl. She's mouthy and defiant in the face of authority—but only to a point. Her seeming power and independence, in comparison to the Damsel (and even the Maiden in the beginning), is a facade. As soon as anyone stronger leans on her, she collapses, sometimes out of fear, but usually simply because she *isn't* strong enough to fight back. And so she resorts to sneaky and manipulative methods for getting what she wants. She "sells" herself by devaluing her worthiness and right to mature into a full-fledged Maiden Arc. Instead, she hides behind the seeming power of her rage.

The Vixen is in a hard place. She refuses to fully accept the authority of those who govern her world (and who probably do protect and provide for her in at least some measure), but she also finds herself unable to accept responsibility for herself by fully claiming her personal sovereignty. In *The Wounded Woman*, Linda Schierse Leonard points out:

> …those daughters who have reacted against the too authoritarian father are likely to have problems accepting their own authority.

THE VIXEN'S POTENTIAL ARCS: POSITIVE AND NEGATIVE

The Vixen offers ripe potential for a dramatic Positive Change Arc. Like all the shadow archetypes, she too will probably show up to at least some degree in any Maiden Arc.

In *Sacred Contracts*, Caroline Myss discusses what she calls the Prostitute as one of four "Archetypes of Survival" within everyone (along with the Child, the Victim, and the Saboteur). She outlines the surprising power of this archetype and its deep potential for growth:

> The Prostitute archetype engages lessons in integrity and the sale or negotiation of one's integrity or spirit due to fears of physical and financial survival or for financial gain. This archetype activates the aspects of the unconscious that are related to seduction and control, whereby you are as capable of buying a controlling interest in another person as

you are in selling your own power. Prostitution should also be understood as the selling of your talents, ideas, and any other expression of the self—or the selling-out of them. This archetype is universal and its core learning relates to the need to birth and refine self-esteem and self-respect.

Of course, the Vixen also holds the potential for stagnation and even deeper devolution into the shadow archetypes. If she fails to use her strength to reorient herself into a powerful Maiden Arc, she might instead follow a tragic Negative Arc in which she becomes even more victimized by the depredations and neglect of her authority figures.

Alternatively, the Vixen might summon the strength to grow—not into the following positive archetype of the Hero, but rather into the subsequent aggressive counter-archetype of the Bully.

Key Points of the Maiden's Shadow Archetypes

Passive Shadow Archetype: Damsel is Submissive (to avoid consequences of Dependence)

Aggressive Shadow Archetype: Vixen is Deceptive (aggressive use of Dependence)

Examples of the Damsel and Vixen Archetypes

Examples of the Damsel and Vixen archetypes include the following.

Damsel

- Paula Alquist in *Gaslight*
- Mrs. de Winter in *Rebecca*
- Neil Perry in *Dead Poets Society*
- Beth in *Little Women*
- Celie Johnson in *The Color Purple*
- Dora Copperfield in *David Copperfield*

WRITING ARCHETYPAL CHARACTER ARCS | 145

- Rapunzel in *Tangled*
- Ophelia in *Hamlet*
- Amy Dorrit in *Little Dorrit*

Vixen

- Gwendolen Harleth in *Daniel Deronda*
- Pip in *Great Expectations*
- Charlotte Flax in *Mermaids*
- Cathy Earnshaw in *Wuthering Heights*
- Antonio Salieri in *Amadeus* (among other aggressive counter-archetypes)
- Lydia Bennet in *Pride & Prejudice*
- Abigail in *The Favourite*
- Edmund Pevensie in *The Lion, the Witch, and the Wardrobe*

"A coward is incapable of exhibiting love;
it is the prerogative of the brave."
—Mahatma Gandhi

10

COWARD AND BULLY

HERE IN THE 21st Century, we often have a confused relationship with the Hero archetype. On the one hand, he is everywhere and we love him and resonate with him. On the other hand, his sheer omnipresence has inevitably highlighted his negative counter-archetypes in almost equal force. This is because wherever we find a would-be Hero, we also find the potential for his regression into the Coward and the Bully.

This is not because the Hero is more flawed than any of the other transformative archetypes, since every positive archetype is partnered with a polarity of passive/aggressive shadow archetypes. However, the Hero's negative archetypes are particularly interesting (and cautionary) simply because of the profound and implicit pervasiveness of the Hero's Journey in the literature and film of the last century. We are perhaps more apt to recognize the latent problems within the Hero Arc simply because those problems are often the very ones that stymie us personally and culturally.

In their classic examination of masculine archetypes, *King, Warrior, Magician, Lover*, Robert Moore and Douglas Gillette point out the inherent, if comparative, immaturity found within the Hero Arc:

There is much confusion about the archetype of the Hero. It is generally assumed that the heroic approach to life, or to a task, is the noblest, but this is only partly true. The Hero is, in fact, only an advanced form of Boy psychology—the most advanced form, the peak, actually, of the masculine energies of the boy, the archetype that characterizes the best in the adolescent stage of development. Yet it is immature, and when it is carried over into adulthood as the governing archetype, it blocks men from full maturity.

As we explored in Chapter 3, this archetype is only the second in a cycle of six. It is the final journey of the "youthful" stage of life, which may be thought of as life's First Act. Therefore, the arc itself is fundamentally about growing up in the fullest sense—not just individuating (which should be accomplished within the preceding Maiden Arc), but now responsibly reintegrating into society as a full-fledged adult.

It is an arc that comes for us all at some point—but one that, despite its prevalence, is misunderstood by modern society simply because we do not always understand what comes next (i.e., the mature "adult" arcs of Queen and King). If the Hero fails to complete his transformation into the mature arcs of life's Second Act, he is very likely to instead transition sideways into his negative shadow archetypes—the Coward and the Bully. The Coward represents the passive polarity within the Hero's shadow, the Bully the aggressive polarity.

THE COWARD: A PASSIVE REFUSAL TO TAKE RESPONSIBILITY

We find the presence of the Coward already implicit within the beginning of every Hero Arc. However much the Hero may long for adventure in "the great wide somewhere," he is not ready to unequivocally volunteer. In the very beginning of his journey, he will display his immaturity via his laziness, complacency, or even outright cowardice. Like Luke Skywalker at the beginning of his journey, he may whine and gripe about his meaningless life in the middle of nowhere, but he won't

WRITING ARCHETYPAL CHARACTER ARCS | 151

summon the courage to leave it until the Call to Adventure arrives (and even then he will start out refusing it, at least symbolically).

There are good reasons for this. However much humans may *need* to grow and mature, our entire concept of survival is built around maintaining a status quo. This is why the Inciting Event and First Plot Point in a story, which force the Hero out of his Normal World, are inevitably "bolts from the blue." They signify the arrival of conflict from *outside* the Hero's safe world.

Not everyone in the story, or in real life, will welcome this. This is normal—indeed, archetypal. Part of the Hero Arc lies within the Hero's own inner struggle *against* the Coward. Only if the Hero's initial Refusal of the Call is not quickly overcome will the Coward begin to prevail.

Like the Damsel before him, the Coward often hides behind a guise of seeming wisdom and maturity. Why take risks? Why not let *others* endanger themselves for the greater good? After all, somebody should stay behind and take care of things back home.

This, however, is false maturity. Once the Call arrives (whatever its form—mythic or modern), it is not the Hero's role to hold the fort. That task belongs to others (i.e., the Queen and the King). If he chooses to ignore this proper ordering of responsibility, he will be doing it for selfish reasons and not for the good of his community. The irony is that he will eventually suffer for it just as much as if he chose to risk all.

THE COWARD'S POTENTIAL ARCS: POSITIVE AND NEGATIVE

As noted, the Coward is already a kernel within the Hero Arc, just waiting to sprout into something better. In many ways the beliefs of the Coward comprise the Lie the Hero Believes—and which the Hero will overcome within a Positive Change Arc.

It should be noted his cowardice may also be projected outward and represented by supporting characters. Allowing supporting characters to "act out" parts of the protagonist's inner self is also a deeply powerful thematic presentation. We can see this in such stories as the Harry Potter movies, in which Harry's lovable best friend Ron Weasley usually represents the Coward, even though he inevitably redeems himself at the end of every installment. In *Star Wars*, the Coward is represented by Threepio, who is always the "voice of caution."

If the Coward does not summon enough courage to embrace his journey (whether at the very beginning of the story or later after he has been thrust upon it against his will), he will fall prey to one of two possible fates.

He might cling ever tighter to his fear and immaturity, which will stultify his growth. Even if life's chronology pushes him ahead into later forms of adulthood and elderhood, he will remain frozen in the passive archetypes—Snow Queen, Puppet, Hermit, and Miser.

The second possibility is that he will pluck up just enough resolve to face his challenges head-on. In so doing, he will discover that he does, in fact, possess more personal power than he realized. But, in this instance too, his forward progression stalls. Instead of using this power to arc into the love and social responsibility of a full-blown Hero, he will instead use this power selfishly (and ultimately still from a place of fear) by turning into the Bully.

THE BULLY: AN AGGRESSIVE REFUSAL TO TAKE RESPONSIBILITY

At first glance, the Bully can seem powerful—more powerful even than the true Hero. But like all aggressive polarities within the shadow archetypes, his power contains a fatal weakness. It is "stuck"—brittle—instead of free-flowing and transformative like the Hero's.

In many ways, the Bully is the *true* shadow form of the Hero. Unlike the Coward, the Bully may well have gotten at least a passing grade on individuating from his authority figures in

WRITING ARCHETYPAL CHARACTER ARCS | 153

the previous arc. But like the Coward, he has stalled out in reintegrating into society in a healthy and responsible way. More than that, he has in fact blocked himself (and/or been obstructed by equally regressive social influences) from doing so. If the Hero represents an arc *into* love, the Bully is ultimately an archetype stuck in hatred.

Deep down, the Bully has embraced a societal wound in a way that not only prevents his healing and growth, but also causes him to fear and resent the idea of reintegration into a larger community. Even when he is surrounded with minions, he stands apart from the cycle of life. Like all aggressive archetypes, he avoids the painful challenges of true growth and instead tries to control reality. As so often happens in cycles of abuse, he becomes the very thing he himself fears and hates.

THE BULLY'S POTENTIAL ARCS: POSITIVE AND NEGATIVE

There is always hope. As with all shadow archetypes, the Bully is not inevitably lost. Indeed, his retained flicker of personal power and his refusal to completely surrender it to those more powerful than himself signals the potential for positive transformation.

Any ultimately transformative Hero Arc may start out emphasizing the Bully side of the character's polarity. Although this can present challenges for the author (and the readers), since the Bully is often unlikable as a character, it does offer the opportunity for a deep arc.

Of course, the fight for his better self may *not* end triumphantly, and the Bully may instead arc more deeply into aggression by rejecting the assimilation of love that is found at the end of a true Hero Arc.

An unredeemed Bully will only abandon his aggressive actions if they prove personally destructive in the external conflict. In this case, it is possible he may lose his willpower and resolve, instead reverting to the passive Coward. Indeed, because the Coward's fear (of life, love, and power) lies at the heart of the Bully archetype, the Coward is always with him to some degree.

Key Points of the Hero's Shadow Archetypes

Passive Shadow Archetype: Coward is Ineffectual (to avoid consequences of Courage)

Aggressive Shadow Archetype: Bully is Destructive (aggressive use of Courage)

Examples of the Coward and Bully Archetypes

Examples of the Coward and Bully archetypes include the following.

Coward

- The Narrator in *Fight Club*
- The Cowardly Lion in *The Wizard of Oz*
- Threepio in *Star Wars*
- Paris in *Troy*
- Edmund Sparkler in *Little Dorrit*
- Richard Carstone in *Bleak House*
- Lambert in *Alien*

Bully

- Thor Odinson in *Thor*
- John Bender in *The Breakfast Club*
- Draco Malfoy in *Harry Potter*
- Regina George in *Mean Girls*
- Fannie Dorrit in *Little Dorrit*
- Gaston in *Beauty & the Beast*
- Sid Phillips in *Toy Story*
- Emily in *The Devil Wears Prada*
- Mary Crawley in *Downton Abbey* (early seasons)
- Liberty Valance in *The Man Who Shot Liberty Valance*

"I love you so much that nothing can matter to me—not even you... Only my love—not your answer. Not even your indifference."
—Ayn Rand

11

SNOW QUEEN AND SORCERESS

A CHARACTER WHO makes it through the Hero Arc is a character who has graduated into a brave new world—the Second Act of the life cycle of archetypal character arcs. This section of life, which deals with questions of relationships and power, begins with the first of the "mature" arcs—that of the Queen. Like all positive archetypes, the Queen's potential for further transformation is "shadowed" by the possibility of her slipping instead into either of two counter-archetypes—the Snow Queen or the Sorceress. The Snow Queen represents the passive polarity within the Queen's shadow; the Sorceress represents the aggressive polarity.

As we saw in Chapter 4, the Queen's journey is characterized not just by the external antagonists she faces in bringing order to her Kingdom, but also by her personal inner struggle against the lure of her own shadow archetypes.

Instead of rising up to protect her family (whether literal or symbolic), she may freeze into the selfish and numb passivity of the Snow Queen. The Snow Queen represents someone who is unable to muster the courage and strength to protect those she loves. Largely, this is because she did not properly learn the lessons of the First Act in gaining the ability to protect and care for *herself*.

Alternatively, it is also possible the Queen may succumb to the alluring but false power of her aggressive form—the

Sorceress. In so doing, she forfeits her true responsibility of becoming a selfless leader to those she loves. Instead, she vampirically manipulates those in her charge in order to meet her own needs.

By the time we reach the archetypal character arcs of the Second Act, we often start seeing some familiar faces from the previous arcs showing up in supporting roles. Here, it's the Maiden and the Hero. Not surprisingly, the negative forms of the Queen (and all later archetypes) are almost inevitably the villains in the younger arcs. The Snow Queen and particularly the Sorceress most frequently turn up in the Maiden Arc, symbolically representing the Too-Good Mother or Devouring Mother or Evil Stepmother from which the young person must individuate.

These negative counter-archetypes stand in stark contrast to the nurturing and growth-encouraging potential of a true Queen—who overcomes her own insecurities in order to foster the growth arcs of her young wards. Part of the Queen's struggle is simply to understand the negative potential within her own arc, by recognizing the signs of the Snow Queen and Sorceress.

The Snow Queen: A Passive Refusal to Fight for What She Loves

The Snow Queen is one of the saddest archetypes. She is still relatively young, still in the first half of her life. But life itself seems to already have left her. She moves through life as if through a fog, and she is not the only one who suffers as a result.

The chronology of her life has pushed her along life's path to some practical degree. She's no longer a Damsel, living with her parents. She has perhaps even sketched what looks, on the outside, to be a Hero Arc. Indeed, the difference between someone who has truly completed the Hero Arc by individuating into a mature adult versus someone who is "only acting the part" may be largely internal. Usually, it has to do almost entirely with whether or not the character took the *true* quest her heart called her to take, or whether she simply took the passive road—the Coward's road—by sleepwalking down the path laid out before her by others.

She is now at the stage of her life when she is expected to be "grown up." As an adult, she is responsible to other people and specifically to the younger people who are rising up behind her. However, because she has not properly completed her own initiations, she not only has little to give, but in her heart of hearts she still sees *herself* as that fair Damsel who must be taken care of.

As with all the passive polarities, she is governed by fear. What she most fears is love. However much she may crave it, she can never let it fully in because it demands too much—too much maturity, too much responsibility, too much reality.

When the threat comes to her Kingdom and her family, she is unequipped to rise to its challenges. At best, she categorizes herself with her children, begging that she too should be saved and taken care of by someone else. At worst, she lets the Invaders steal away her children in the hope that at least she might be left in peace.

THE SNOW QUEEN'S POTENTIAL ARCS: POSITIVE AND NEGATIVE

The Snow (or Ice) Queen of fairy and folk tale is often portrayed as a beautiful woman living alone in a palace of ice. If she is to be redeemed, she must be rescued (often by children or a young Hero) who can warm her frozen heart with a revelation of love.

Right there, we can see the deep and beautiful potential within the Snow Queen for a Positive Arc into a true Queen. The lesson she missed in failing to complete the previous Hero Arc was, in a word, love. Before she can go on to claim the ruling principle of the true Queen—i.e., order—she must first be thawed by that love.

As indicated in the old tales, she may be saved from herself by her own children, who she then will save from larger threats against the Kingdom. Or she may be saved by the love of a questing Hero who, within his own arc, submits his power to her as the person in his life for whom he is finally willing to fight and die.

The Snow Queen may also remain inured within her passivity, and her story may spiral into deep tragedy as her children, or whomever she is responsible for, are plunged into their own tragedies (or at least difficulties) through her lack of responsibility. Whether through the depredations of Invaders or because her family simply grows up enough to move on without her, the end of her story will find her all alone.

Worse still, she may summon the energy to rise out of her passivity only to hurtle into the full-on destructive manipulation of her aggressive polarity—the Sorceress.

The Sorceress: An Aggressive Refusal to Do What Is Best for What She Loves

In the Snow Queen, we find the shadow archetype of someone who, even in midlife, has not yet found a true and nourishing flow of love. We see this same core problem in the Sorceress, but unlike her passive partner, the Sorceress is at least trying to take control of her situation and get her needs met—however misguidedly.

In the online article "How Not to Fall in Love with the Anima/Animus," Sinéad Donohoe makes an interesting note that can be seen to apply to this particular shadow archetype:

> As she appears in myth, the temptress is the damsel whose cries for rescue went unheeded, and who has been allowed to perish.

The Sorceress is the Vixen who wasn't given the support and resources she needed to healthily individuate from her birth family, just as she is also the Bully who used whatever power was available to meet personal needs. Now in the Second Act of her life cycle, she finally has some freedom from and power

WRITING ARCHETYPAL CHARACTER ARCS | 163

over others. But due to her fundamental feeling of lack and her distrust of true love, she uses any and all means at her disposal to meet her needs by securing resources from others. At this point, many of the people she manipulates are those who are more vulnerable than she is and for whom she herself is now responsible in some way.

In *The Hero Within*, in reference to the shadow form of what she calls "the Altruist," Carol S. Pearson offers examples of how this Sorceress energy can manifest in recognizable modern situations:

> [People in the shadow form of] the Altruist ... will be unable—no matter how hard they work at it—to sacrifice truly out of love and care for others, and their sacrifice will not be transformative. If they sacrifice for their children, the children must then pay and pay and pay—by being appropriately grateful, by living the life the parents wish they had lived, in short, by sacrificing their own lives in return. It is this pseudo-sacrifice, which really is a form of manipulation, that has given sacrifice a bad name.

However unconsciously, the Sorceress preys upon her dependents while they are young and then tries to trap them in a perpetual dependence on her by preventing them from taking their own individuating arcs of Maiden and Hero.

THE SORCERESS'S POTENTIAL ARCS: POSITIVE AND NEGATIVE

The deeper a character gets into the life arcs' shadow archetypes, the harder it can be to pull free. But redemption is always possible, although it can mean returning to previous Positive Arcs that were never properly completed.

Like all the aggressive polarities, the Sorceress's deep pit of problems offers the opportunity for huge Positive Arcs. If she can somehow find the courage to recognize, acknowledge, and address her own deeply entrenched negative patterns, she may yet find the strength to rise into the true Queen Arc of responsible leadership. This can be the powerful midlife story of someone who has always followed the company line, to her own detriment, only to realize she's living someone else's life. She chucks it all out the window and finally takes off on the Hero's quest she should have taken many years ago.

However, she may also fail to break her own destructive patterns. She may remain a Sorceress—an antagonist to other people's own growth arcs—or she may devolve further into a full-blown despot. By "upping" her power from mere manipulation to full-on oppression, she can take a shadow version of the Queen Arc and end up, not a responsible and loving King, but a hideous and death-dealing Tyrant.

Key Points of the Queen's Shadow Archetypes

Passive Shadow Archetype: Snow Queen is Defensive (to avoid consequences of Love)

Aggressive Shadow Archetype: Sorceress is Manipulative/Vampiric (aggressive use of Love)

Examples of Snow Queen and Sorceress Archetypes

Examples of the Snow Queen and Sorceress archetypes include the following.

Snow Queen

- Lady Dedlock in *Bleak House*
- Mary Crawley in *Downton Abbey* (she also displays Bully qualities, as noted in the previous chapter, but she exhibits more of the Snow Queen as she gets older)
- Jon Snow in *Game of Thrones* (he eventually overcomes his Snow Queen tendencies to become a leader)
- Blanche DuBois in *A Streetcar Named Desire*
- Mr. Darcy in *Pride & Prejudice*

Sorceress

- Tai-Lung in *Kung-Fu Panda*
- Loki in *Thor*
- Scarlett O'Hara in *Gone With the Wind*
- Joan Crawford in *Mommie Dearest*
- Commodus in *Gladiator*
- Mrs. Elton in *Emma*
- Cersei Lannister in *Game of Thrones*
- Rodmilla de Ghent (Evil Step-Mother) in *Ever After*
- Mrs. Bennett in *Pride & Prejudice*
- Mrs. Gibson in *Wives & Daughters*

"Our soul is sometimes a king,
sometimes a tyrant.
An uncontrolled, over-indulged soul
is turned from a king
to the most-feared tyrant."
—Seneca

12

PUPPET AND TYRANT

THROUGHOUT THE PROGRESSION of the six archetypal character arcs, we have seen a steady progression of the character's power. As explored in the positive King Arc in Chapter 5, this final midlife arc represents the height of temporal power. The King is someone who wields a vast amount of influence not just over his own life or within his personal relationships, but over extended numbers of people. In mythological terms, he rules over a Kingdom, but more practically, his empire could be anything from a large family to a company.

In short, he's the boss. He knows it. Everybody knows it. Whether literally or symbolically, he holds within his hand the power of life and death over his subjects. Will he wield that power responsibly in a way that brings life to the Kingdom? The answer depends on whether he is centered within his positive aspect of King, or whether he is gripped by his shadow archetypes of Puppet and Tyrant. The Puppet represents the passive polarity within the King's shadow; the Tyrant represents the aggressive polarity.

Along with the growing power that accumulates as a character progresses farther into the life arcs, so too the stakes rise proportionately. The more power the character accumulates, the greater his ability to do good to others—or evil. This evil inevitably results from a stagnation of growth. It could happen because a character was thrust into a position of leadership even though he failed to properly complete previous initiations. Or it could be he worked his way up through the aggressive archetypes, building his Kingdom on the backs of those he selfishly oppressed along the way.

It's also possible for someone to responsibly and authentically reach an archetype, only to stall out in his growth by over-identifying with his current archetype. In *King, Warrior, Magician, Lover*, Robert Moore and Douglas Gillette refer to this as being "possessed" by an archetype. They indicate how the King archetype, particularly, may be forced into a shadow version of his own arc—still facing the propitiatory sacrifice demanded of him, but doing so unwillingly:

> As Sir James Frazer and others have observed, kings in the ancient world were often ritually killed when their ability to live out the King archetype began to fail.... The danger for men who become possessed by this energy is that they too will fulfill the ancient pattern and die prematurely.

It is no coincidence that the negative archetypes of later arcs often act as antagonists to the younger arcs. A King gone bad makes a formidable foe, creating the opportunity for a story with huge stakes. He shows up most often in Hero stories (in which the Hero's quest may be about trying to "heal" the Sick King—see Chapter 24) and Queen stories (in which the Queen must grow into a leader worthy of responsibly replacing the unfit King—see Chapter 25). In *The Hero With a Thousand Faces*, Joseph Campbell frequently refers to this villain as the "tyrant ogre" or "Holdfast"—the representative of a stalled status quo.

Like all the negative archetypes, the Puppet and the Tyrant represent a personal failure to examine the Lies the Character Believes, to lean into growth, and to accept the next level of maturity and responsibility within one's life.

The Puppet: A Passive Refusal to Be a True Servant-Leader

The passive archetypes represent missed steps within the character's growth. They "skipped a grade"—but not in a good way. The farther they get into life, the more egregious this deficiency becomes, both for themselves and for others. The Puppet is a particularly potent example.

As the passive polarity within the King's negative counter-archetypes, the Puppet necessarily represents a character who at least nominally holds a great deal of power. Unfortunately, he lacks the strength, ability, or perhaps even desire to wield that power. He may have been born to the power, or he may have fostered a seeming sense of "maturity" to the point that he sneakily advanced beyond his actual capabilities. Regardless exactly how he manifests, the Puppet is someone who wields his power only randomly and to his own benefit. Either he is content to fob off all true responsibilities onto others, or he himself is at the mercy of someone more powerful (likely a Tyrant or a Sorcerer).

The character will almost inevitably display a "spoiled brat" sense of entitlement that reveals his true level of immaturity. This puerility is exceedingly dangerous to others due to the power with which it is paired. As with all the passive shadow archetypes, it represents a deep sense of fear and insecurity within the Puppet himself. He isn't truly powerful; he just *wields* power.

In modern storytelling, a clear example can be found in the *Game of Thrones* characters Joffrey and Tommen Baratheon. Even though psychotic Joffrey *wants* to be a Tyrant, both he and later his well-intentioned little brother Tommen are obviously Puppets to their Tyrant grandfather Tywin Lannister. Both are Puppets purely for the reason that they were thrust into positions of power without having properly arced into the true maturity of the King, both being only teenagers.

The Puppet's Potential Arcs: Positive and Negative

It is always possible for a passive archetype to rise to the challenge and learn the lessons of its related Positive Arc. However, the farther along a character is within the chronological arcs, the more likely he will have to *go back* to fulfill previous archetypes first. This leveling up can be done all within the same story in a relatively short amount of time. But the degree of transformation will be tremendous.

If the Puppet's primary problem is that he is not chronologically advanced into the proper placement of the King Arc (such as in the case of the Baratheon princes in *Game of Thrones*), his best path of growth is a return to his properly timed arc (i.e., Maiden or Hero).

However, the more powerful a character is, the harder it can be to let go of that power—however stagnated or unhealthy it may be for him personally. Only someone brave enough to undergo an extraordinary transformation will be able to release his ill-gotten temporal power, even if that power is merely nominal as in the case of the Puppet.

Therefore, it is more likely the Puppet will refuse to evolve and will end his story as a tragedy in the midst of the Kingdom he could not and would not protect. Worse still, he may instead choose to seize more power, refusing to step aside even when it is time and instead using his position to oppress his Kingdom as the Tyrant.

The Tyrant: An Aggressive Refusal to Be a True Servant-Leader

The Tyrant is a chillingly well-known archetype—historically, globally, and personally. Humans have a hard enough time wielding power, much less surrendering it—and surrender is the heart of a true King Arc.

The Tyrant never surrenders. The Tyrant will take his power to the grave—and his Kingdom with him. However well he

WRITING ARCHETYPAL CHARACTER ARCS | 173

may manage the actual affairs of the Kingdom (and many Tyrants *do* prove to be brilliant managers), he is ultimately a curse upon his Kingdom and his subjects. The true King steps aside to make room for new life; the Tyrant blocks that life and ultimately can give his Kingdom only death, even if he does not directly desire such.

Profound unhealth governs and emerges from the Tyrant's refusal to sacrifice for his Kingdom. The Tyrant proves his own distrustful and (ironically) immature relationship to power by doing everything he can to hang on to everything he's got. Because the King Arc is all about surrendering power and prestige as a preparation for the descent into the Underworld of elderhood (and, eventually, the end of life), the Tyrant's rejection of this arc is ultimately an attempt to reject his own mortality. The unrepentant Tyrant, then, is always doomed.

THE TYRANT'S POTENTIAL ARCS: POSITIVE AND NEGATIVE

The responsibilities of the King are tricky ones. He must constantly weigh such questions as "How much power is too much?" and "Where have I the right to rule over my subjects—and where am I overstepping?" Every King will make mistakes. Present within every positive King is always the shadow of the Tyrant. As a result, there is also always the potential for a return to the King in every Tyrant (especially if he has proven himself faithful in his earlier arcs).

Because the King Arc symbolically and sometimes literally ends with his death, it is not uncommon for a repentant Tyrant to also end by giving his life for his Kingdom. Depending on how far gone he is within the negative archetype, this may be the best he can hope for in trying to repair his own mistakes.

On the other hand, he may also perish in less admirable circumstances. If the Tyrant refuses to relinquish power and remains stubbornly in his unregenerative patterns, a younger Hero or Queen may arise to remove his stain from upon the Kingdom. (For example, Gillette and Moore reference the biblical story of King David replacing the Tyrant Saul.)

If the Tyrant is exceedingly powerful, and if he is not confronted by Heroes or Queens strong enough to dethrone him, the inevitable cycle of life may still push him off his throne at some point. Old age will claim him one way or another. If he cannot gracefully accept the transition from King to Crone, he is likely instead to devolve into the manipulative powers of the Witch, working behind the scenes, before eventually returning to the world's stage as the even more destructive Sorcerer.

KEY POINTS OF THE KING'S SHADOW ARCHETYPES

Passive Shadow Archetype: Puppet is Irresponsible (to avoid consequences of Power)

Aggressive Shadow Archetype: Tyrant is Oppressive (aggressive use of Power)

EXAMPLES OF THE PUPPET AND TYRANT ARCHETYPES

Examples of the Puppet and Tyrant archetypes include the following.

Puppet

- Joffrey and Tommen Baratheon in *Game of Thrones*
- Theoden in *The Two Towers*
- Tsarina Alexandra in *Rasputin and the Empress*
- Nels Olson in *The Little House on the Prairie*
- Prince John in *Robin Hood*
- Mr. Bennett in *Pride & Prejudice*
- King Louis XIII in *The Musketeers*

Tyrant

- Heathcliff in *Wuthering Heights*
- Michael Corleone in *The Godfather*
- Tywin Lannister in *Game of Thrones*
- Daenerys Targaryen in *Game of Thrones* (second half)
- Miranda Priestley in *The Devil Wears Prada*

- Old Man Potter in *It's a Wonderful Life*
- Miss Minchin in *A Little Princess*
- Catherine de Burgh in *Pride & Prejudice*
- Edward Rochester in *Jane Eyre*
- Mrs. Merdle in *Little Dorrit*
- Professor Delores Umbridge in *Harry Potter and the Order of the Phoenix*
- Yubaba in *Spirited Away*
- Tom Dunson in *Red River*
- Cardinal Richelieu in *The Musketeers*

"A fine line separates the weary recluse from the fearful hermit. Finer still is the line between hermit and bitter misanthrope."
—Dean Koontz

13

HERMIT AND WITCH

THE FINAL TWO archetypal character arcs within the life cycle signal a distinct departure from the realm of the known. After sacrificing for the Kingdom at the end of the King Arc, the seemingly diminished Crone leaves behind the "real" world of Kingdom and throne to instead enter the spooky forests and liminal hinterlands of elderhood. Symbolically, the final two Positive Arcs—Crone and Mage—are decidedly more supernatural than those that preceded.

In archetypal and mythic stories, we see this shift represented by these characters' ability to perform "magic." This magic can represent the potential for a deeper spirituality, but it also certainly represents the accumulated life experience, knowledge, and wisdom of the characters' arcs up until this point. The two arcs prior to that of the Crone—the Queen and the King—were focused on issues of power. As such, a character who has successfully completed those arcs will have a wily understanding of power that outstrips even the physically powerful youths of the earlier arcs. (We see this delightfully represented in the film *Secondhand Lions*, in which Robert Duvall's Crone character handily beats up a gang of Bullies—then takes them home to doctor their black eyes and offer them his initiatory speech about "how to be a man.")

As discussed in Chapter 6, the Crone offers the potential for a profound arc into the deeper mysteries of Life and Death.

It is, however, a deeply fraught archetype. As the structural representation of life's Third Plot Point (often called the "Low Moment" or the "Dark Night of the Soul" or simply "Death/Rebirth"), the Crone successfully completes her King Arc only to be faced with the most frightening existential challenge of her long life.

The Crone, all alone in her hut in the woods, represents a time of withdrawal from the world. This is so she can integrate the great losses and lessons she has taken away from her life's Second Act period. That she can successfully mourn and integrate these lessons is not a given. If she cannot come to peace with the life she has so far lived, her regrets about what she might not have done or what she can no longer do, and her inevitably encroaching death—she may easily slide into one or both of her negative counter-archetypes of Hermit and Wicked Witch. The Hermit represents the passive polarity within the Crone's shadow; the Witch represents the aggressive polarity.

THE HERMIT: A PASSIVE REJECTION OF BOTH LIFE AND DEATH

In many ways, the Hermit is an almost inevitable beat within the Crone's "resurrection" after dying for the Kingdom and departing it in her previous arc. It is symbolically important that the Crone lives alone in a hut in the woods and often scares away (intentionally or unintentionally) anyone who might disturb her. This is because her first steps are those of healing, processing, and integrating. The Death symbolized in the end of the King Arc is profound, both in itself (represented perhaps by a person's forced retirement from a beloved occupation) and in its foreshadowing of literal Death. That's a *lot*. If the Crone is to have any chance of truly maturing into her full positive potential, she must first make peace with what she has lost. And she will likely do this best in solitude.

However, the danger (especially if she is indeed chronologically in the Third Act of her life) is that she may *stay* in solitude. The struggle to rise once more from her warm bed or her sunny rocking chair may be too great. Her grief over the life she has lost may seem insurmountable. This may be even more true if she has struggled with passive archetypes all her life and therefore must not only mourn the youth she has lost but confront regrets for a life that now seems unlived.

The Hermit's central temptation is simply that of... giving up. Although she may have thirty or more years yet to live, she can know with certainty that the greater part of her life is now behind her. In the face of her waning physical power, she may succumb to the question: "What's the point?" Even when her next Call to Adventure arrives in the form of a Maiden or Hero needing her guidance, she may choose simply to roll over, turn her face to the wall, and refuse to reintegrate with a Kingdom that desperately needs her wisdom and her capacity to initiate the young.

THE HERMIT'S POTENTIAL ARCS: POSITIVE AND NEGATIVE

In many ways, the Crone Arc is *about* rising above the somnolent lure of the Hermit. There is a great triumph in stories of characters who overcome what is in many ways the greatest antagonist any of us will ever face in the actual living of our lives. To do so, the Hermit must be willing to surrender many of her old identities and viewpoints.

She can no longer fixate on the future as she did in younger arcs. Now she must ground herself in the present. Within this deep self-acceptance and love, the Crone may then also find the capacity for an even deeper love of the Kingdom and its young occupants.

If, however, the Hermit cannot rise from her bed of self-pity, regret, and lethargy, she may find her life force simply fading away. She may not live out the full remainder of her life expectancy, or if she does, she may no longer "live" but simply "exist."

Tragically, another potential shadow arc is that from Hermit to Wicked Witch. In some ways, this is a positive transition, since it at least signals a revival of purpose and liveliness. But this is also a deeply destructive transition, since it signals that the character has not overcome her resentment or bitterness about her fate—and will turn upon the very young people she is meant to guide and protect.

The Wicked Witch: An Aggressive Rejection of Both Life and Death

Someone willing to fully embody the positive Crone Arc is one who will come to fully align herself with Life—and to use her great wisdom and experience to guide the young people into their own archetypal life journeys. If, however, the archetype turns into the aggressive polarity of the Wicked Witch, she will instead align herself with Death—and not in a natural way. Since she has failed to visit and return from the Underworld as the fulfillment of her Crone Arc, she will also fail to possess a full and generative understanding of Death. To her, Death is something to be feared, and she wields this fear against others.

Prosaically, the Witch is simply an older person who refuses the responsibilities of elderhood and instead manipulates and bullies those around her in order to get her needs met. More metaphorically, the Witch is a frequent symbolic antagonist in many types of stories. We recognize her by her hatred for life, especially the life that is represented by the young of the Kingdom. As in *Snow White*, the Witch may often be presented as an initially beautiful Queen—only to reveal her true hideousness in that she is feeding off the life force of the Kingdom's young and beautiful Maidens.

In some ways, the Witch seems to be far more powerful than the Crone (at least at the beginning of the Crone Arc), but this can be because in claiming her aggressive power she has "gotten ahead of herself." The aggressive shadow archetypes often share significant similarities with the subsequent positive archetypes. This is because the aggressive archetypes are always grasping for more power. They have the advantage over the passive archetypes of at least wanting to progress, but they are unwilling and/or have not understood how to do so from a place of health and centeredness.

WRITING ARCHETYPAL CHARACTER ARCS | 183

THE WITCH'S POTENTIAL ARCS: POSITIVE AND NEGATIVE

If the character has not fully entrenched herself in the Witch's bitterness and hatred of life (i.e., has not become "possessed" by the archetype), she may yet integrate her massive transition from the mature arcs of her life's Second Act into the elder arcs of her life's Third Act. This is a tricky space, since once a character fully inhabits her bitterness—especially since she now has comparatively little time left in which to resolve it—she may not be able to pull herself out.

Within film and literature, we don't often see redemptive ends for characters who have fully embodied the Witch archetype (which it should go without saying by this point is distinct from a character who may *be* a witch—such as Glinda in *The Wizard of Oz*). This is because the aggressive negative archetypes grow successively *more* aggressive and *more* negative as they go. It's hard enough to redeem a full-blown Tyrant. As mentioned in the previous chapter, "redeemed" Tyrants almost always die in the end. It grows even harder to redeem the aggressive archetypes of the Third Act.

Therefore, on the less happy side, the Witch may end her story unchanged, having wreaked varying degrees of havoc upon the world around her. If her children and grandchildren—her Maidens, Heroes, Queens, and Kings—cannot escape her influence, they may well be doomed (as shown in Meryl Streep's role as an embittered and malicious matriarch in *August: Osage County*).

It is also possible the Witch may summon enough power and longevity to "advance" one more time into the pinnacle of aggressive power—the Mage's aggressive counter-archetype of Sorcerer. This most mystical of all aggressive archetypes isn't often represented in realistic literature; in fantasy, it is almost inevitably personified as evil incarnate. It's not a good way to go out!

Key Points of the Crone's Shadow Archetypes

Passive Shadow Archetype: Hermit is Misanthropic (to avoid consequences of Insight)

Aggressive Shadow Archetype: Witch is Punitive (aggressive use of Insight)

Examples of the Hermit and Witch Archetypes

Examples of the Hermit and Witch archetypes include the following.

Hermit

- Elderly Margaret Thatcher in beginning of *The Iron Lady*
- Matthew and Marilla Cuthbert in beginning of *Anne of Green Gables*
- Silas Marner in beginning of *Silas Marner*
- Aunt March in *Little Women*
- Mrs. Snow in *Pollyanna*
- Miss Havisham in *Great Expectations*

Witch

- Wicked Witch of the West in *The Wizard of Oz*
- Witch of the Waste in *Howl's Moving Castle*
- Norma Desmond in *Sunset Boulevard*
- Fagin in *Oliver Twist*
- Violet Weston in *August: Osage County*
- Sister Aloysius Beauvier in *Doubt*
- Captain Ahab in *Moby Dick*
- Mr. Dorrit in *Little Dorrit*

"What greater evil could you wish a miser
than long life?"
—Syrus Publilius

14

MISER AND SORCERER

STRUCTURALLY SPEAKING, IT is always a story's end—its Climactic Moment—that tells us what it is about. The Climactic Moment concludes the external plot by telling us who "wins." It also implicitly ends the protagonist's arc by showing us whether the character succeeded in arcing positively and helping others to do the same, or if the character failed to overcome inner challenges and "level up."

The Mage Arc is the final moment in the story of the life cycle. As the Climactic Moment, it reveals the ultimate theme of a life, now that we finally see the entire big picture. It is the final piece that allows the larger mosaic to reveal its meaning.

Will the character complete this final arc positively, die a good death, and leave a powerful legacy to the descendants? Or will the character succumb in the end to the powerful temptations and struggles of either of the potential negative shadow archetypes—the Miser or the Sorcerer? The Miser, of course, represents the passive polarity within the Mage's shadow; the Sorcerer represents the aggressive polarity.

If the challenges of the Maiden and Hero Arcs seemed hard at first, they now look small indeed in comparison to the stakes of the Mage Arc. There is a reason so few people reach this arc much less fulfill it. The good news for the Mage is that by this point in his long and full life, he has gained a treasure trove of resources. He could not have advanced so far had he not proven himself strong enough to push through previous arcs and learn at least some of their lessons.

But, as always, whether or not the Mage will fulfill a beneficial role in relationship to society remains a final choice. Depending in large part on how well he managed the resources won in his previous arcs, he may now find himself prone to slipping into his negative forms as either a reclusive and selfish Miser who hoards his life's wisdom or a megalomaniacal despot who not only has the power to rule (as does a Tyrant) but also the power to obscenely manipulate others via his deep understanding of reality.

The heart of a positive Mage Arc is the ability to surrender not just power, but ultimately life itself. If he cannot master this capitulation, he will forfeit his responsibilities of guiding and initiating the young and will end instead by trying to control the fate of the Kingdom according to his personal pleasure.

The Miser: A Passive Hoarding of Power

As a natural progression of the Crone's passive counter-archetype of the Hermit, the Miser is one who has failed to overcome the Third Act's central challenge of bitterness toward his mortal fate. Instead, his bitterness has only grown with the years. He sees himself as unjustly banished from the Kingdom to which he gave long years of good service. He has devolved from being antisocial to being truly misanthropic. He disdains society and therefore young life itself, believing no one is worthy of him and his gifts.

Although he may feel a deep and personal bitterness that he should be so treated, in actuality his fate is probably not specifically worse than anyone else's at this stage in life. Whether he realizes it or not, what he is really angry about is the fact of his own mortality. He has amassed so much wisdom and power; he has done so well at life. But, in the end, he will not be able to buy off Death.

And so he punishes the Kingdom (which is always in desperate need of healthy Elders and Mentors) by withdrawing and hoarding everything he has spent his life to gain.

The Miser's Potential Arcs: Positive and Negative

The Miser can be seen to represent the foundational trial of the Mage Arc: the need to surrender. As Yoda, one of our culture's most popular Mage characters, says:

> You must give up everything you fear to lose.

If a Miser can learn to do this, he still has the opportunity to return to center as a healthy Mage and complete his final arc in a positive and life-giving way (literally). As ever, the shadow versions of a positive archetype are always present within the arcs. The passive archetype is active in the First Act of any specific arc, at the point when the protagonist is wrestling with the Call to Adventure and deciding whether he can overcome his own passive and cowardly tendencies in order to take one more journey of the soul.

Archetypally, the Mage/Mentor character is often seen to be either roaming about the Kingdom on his own (like Mary Poppins), or still living in the Crone's hut (like Yoda). Although he has somewhat reintegrated with the Kingdom in his previous arc, he is still separate from it. He lives in the liminal space of elderhood, no longer enmeshed in the wheels of commerce and survival, although still interacting with it.

The Mage's challenge arrives when the Kingdom comes under a supernatural threat (or a natural threat that only the Mage recognizes as having a supernatural aspect). This challenge requires him to embark on one last mission to mentor the young. If he chooses to accept that challenge, he will rise out of the temptation of the Miser and advance positively. If he does not, he may remain the Miser by turning his back on the Kingdom and passively enabling its ultimate destruction (even if all he's refusing is to initiate the young).

Worse yet, he may indeed yet rise up into his full power, only to egoically turn it back upon his own Kingdom. Instead of acting as a Mentor and using his great power to help the Kingdom learn to fight its battles and continue the life cycle, he instead seizes the Kingdom and its inhabitants as playthings by right of his own power.

THE SORCERER: AN AGGRESSIVE ABUSE OF POWER

As the final Positive Arc, the Mage's journey is not about gaining something, as in previous arcs. Rather, it is entirely about letting go. If he refuses to let go and instead attempts to continue gaining power, he will soon find himself in the excessive and aggressive form of his shadow archetype—the Sorcerer.

Like the Mage, the Sorcerer's final antagonist is that of mortality itself. But in seeking to have "power over life," he becomes instead possessed by the death-force. In *The Hero Within*, Carol S. Pearson describes this beautifully in her commentary of Ursula K. LeGuin's fantasy *The Farthest Shore* (adapted, in part, into Studio Ghibli's *Tales of Earthsea* film):

> [The Mage Sparrowhawk] explains that what has caused [the Kingdom to become possessed by death's shadow] is that people desire "power over life," which he calls "greed." The only power worth having, he notes, is not "power over," but "power to" accept life, to allow it in. The desire to control life and death in order to attain immortality creates a void within and throws the cosmos out of balance. Sparrowhawk explains to [the Sorcerer] Cob that "Not all the songs of earth, not all the stars of heaven could fill your emptiness," for Cob, in going for "power over," has lost himself and his true name. [Mages], then, give up the illusion of control to allow life in themselves and in others. When they do so, they right the balance of the universe.

Our other great fantasies of the age also offer us this same powerful contrast between the life-giving balance of the true Mage and the selfish destruction of the Sorcerer. We see Yoda

WRITING ARCHETYPAL CHARACTER ARCS | 193

contrasting Emperor Palpatine in *Star Wars*, Dumbledore contrasting Voldemort in *Harry Potter*, and perhaps most precisely Gandalf contrasting Saruman in *Lord of the Rings*. The latter characters are all death-dealers, determined to amass dark power to themselves at the cost of "lesser" beings.

The Sorcerer not only coerces submission from the Kingdom through his actual power, he also convinces people to willingly follow his wishes by seducing them into their own shadow archetypes.

THE SORCERER'S POTENTIAL ARCS: POSITIVE AND NEGATIVE

In many ways, the Sorcerer represents the ultimate low to which a human being can fall. If he truly embodies this archetype, he is unlikely to find within himself the ability to return to the light. Indeed, he will probably find it difficult to *desire* a return to the light.

In part because he has advanced so far in his dark power, and also in part because his time on earth is running out, he has little to no chance of returning to a final Positive Arc. Only if, miraculously, he can return to a belief that, in Pearson's words, "nothing essential is ever lost," will he be able to reclaim a glimmer of light.

Neither is he likely to arc negatively, because, again, he's out of time. At worst, his story will end with the total destruction of the Kingdom and himself in it. At best, he will either destroy himself through his own hubristic overreach, or the Heroes, Queens, Kings, Crones, and Mages will rise up to overthrow him.

The cycle of life wants always to continue. Even if a terrible Sorcerer rises up, wields great power, and does everything he can (whether consciously or unconsciously) to destroy that cycle by breaking out of his own sacred role of Mage and Mentor, new life and new growth will return to the Kingdom once more like new green grass after a bitter winter.

Key Points of the Mage's Shadow Archetypes

Passive Shadow Archetype: Miser is Selfish (to protect from consequences of Enlightenment)

Aggressive Shadow Archetype: Sorcerer is Evil (aggressive use of Enlightenment)

Examples of the Miser and Sorcerer Archetypes

Examples of the Miser and Sorcerer archetypes include the following.

Miser

- Grendel's mother in *Beowulf*
- Ebenezer Scrooge in (the beginning of) *A Christmas Carol*
- Louis Renault in *Casablanca*
- Frollo in *The Hunchback of Notre Dame*

Sorcerer

- Maleficent in *Sleeping Beauty*
- Jadis the White Witch in *The Lion, the Witch, and the Wardrobe*
- Saruman the White in *The Lord of the Rings*
- Emperor Palpatine in *Star Wars*
- Mr. Tulkinghorn in *Bleak House*
- Voldemort in *Harry Potter and the Order of the Phoenix* (among others)

Part 3: The Six Flat or Resting Archetypes

"Perfection of character is this:
to live each day as if it were your last,
without frenzy, without apathy,
without pretence."
—Marcus Aurelius

15

INTRODUCTION TO THE SIX FLAT OR RESTING ARCHETYPES

IN STUDYING CHARACTER arcs, writers easily recognize Positive Change Arcs and Negative Change Arcs. Somewhat more baffling can be the stories that appear to feature neither. These are stories in which the protagonist does not change or seems to have no character arc at all. How do these stories fit into the discussion of archetypal character arcs?

In my previous book *Creating Character Arcs*, I spoke about two possible answers to the seeming conundrum of the "character with no arc."

One is simply that he or she *doesn't* arc. The protagonist, the supporting cast, and the story world itself all remain relatively unchanged from beginning to end, despite everyone's adventures. Indeed, the very point of their adventures might be to *maintain* a desirable status quo.

The other possibility is that the unchanging protagonist is in fact spearheading a Flat Arc. As the name suggests, this is an arc in which the protagonist—the story's central actor—remains thematically unchanged. Instead, the protagonist uses an understanding of the story's central thematic Truth to catalyze Change Arcs in the supporting characters. (Flat-Arc protagonists are usually positive influences, but if their fixation is on the thematic Lie rather than the Truth, they can also be instrumental in catalyzing Negative Change Arcs for the supporting characters.)

In the first section of this book, we explored the successive Positive Change Arcs of six primary archetypes—the Maiden, the Hero, the Queen, the King, the Crone, and the Mage. Each positive archetype represents a rising above the limitations of its previous archetype in the cycle. As discussed in the book's second section, these six main archetypes also inherently represent a struggle with twelve related "shadow" or negative archetypes—the Damsel/Vixen, the Coward/Bully, the Snow Queen/Sorceress, the Puppet/Tyrant, the Hermit/Witch, and the Miser/Sorcerer.

As unchanging characters, Flat Arc protagonists are equally archetypal, but unlike the six Positive Change Arcs, they do not demonstrate a "journey" from one archetype to another (e.g., Maiden to Hero). Rather, they represent the interstitial period of a character's life, in which the character "rests" between personal transformations. As such, these Flat archetypes are often seen to be helping or teaching other characters some of the same lessons they just learned in their own previously completed arcs.

Six Flat or "Resting" Archetypes

The six flat or resting archetypes look like this:

1. Child (precedes Maiden Arc)

2. Lover (precedes Hero Arc)

3. Parent (precedes Queen Arc)

4. Ruler (precedes King Arc)

5. Elder (precedes Crone Arc)

6. Mentor (precedes Mage Arc)

As you can see, many of these Flat archetypes initially seem synonymous with the Change Arcs that follow (e.g., Ruler/King, Elder/Crone). In some ways, they *are* synonymous, in

WRITING ARCHETYPAL CHARACTER ARCS | 203

large part because each of the Positive Change archetypes begins its First Act within the complacency of the preceding Flat archetype. For example, the King Arc begins with the character clearly a Ruler, even though his arc will be about transforming *out* of that static archetype, requiring him to give up his throne in some way by the end. In contrast, a story that is *about* the Flat archetype is one in which the protagonist will begin and end within the same archetype. If he begins as a Ruler, he will end as a Ruler, still upon his throne in the story's conclusion.

How to Use Flat Archetypes in a Story

Flat Arcs offer the potential to unapologetically present archetypal characters who do what we all want to do—enact meaningful change on the world around us. Although the relative positivity or negativity of that change will depend on whether the protagonist is aligned with the story's thematic Truth or Lie, for the sake of this discussion, we will be assuming the archetypal protagonists featured in these Flat-Arc stories are positive in their alignment with a beneficial Truth. In short, these characters are likely to be *in between* their own Positive Change Arcs.

The hallmark of a Flat Arc (in contrast to a story with "no arc") is that the protagonist is able to create significant change in the surrounding world. The Flat Arc protagonist is the Impact Character in someone else's Positive Change Arc. Particularly within the cycle of the archetypal life arcs, the Flat archetypes represent moments within the protagonist's life in which he or she is able to put to use the lessons learned in previous arcs.

Therefore:

> Adolescence demands the **Child** undertake a coming-of-age initiation as the **Maiden**, who then explores a burgeoning into adulthood as the **Lover**.

> The **Lover** must then embark on the **Hero**'s quest, but comes home from these adventures and settles down to become a **Parent**.

As the children begin reaching maturity, the **Parent** must then rise up as **Queen** to defend and properly lead them as the **Ruler**.

Having been crowned, the **Ruler** may spend years leading the Kingdom, before taking the sacrificial **King** Arc into **Elder**hood.

Now an **Elder**, the character influences subsequent generations on the way to undergoing a full **Crone** Arc that will allow a spiritual leveling up into one of the most archetypal characters of all—the **Mentor**.

As the **Mentor**, the character may then bless the Kingdom one last time before entering the final journey of the **Mage**.

As always, all these titles are symbolic. A character does not literally need to be a parent in order to represent the Parent archetype, anymore than a Mage character must literally be able to work magic. We will discuss this further in subsequent chapters exploring each of the Flat archetypes.

How the Positive Archetypes Relate to the Flat Archetypes

Flat Arc stories are, in fact, Positive Change Arc stories in disguise. Although they seem at first glance to be stories in which there is no arc, this is an illusion. The protagonist doesn't change, but at least one supporting character does.

As such, you can often overlay any appropriate Positive Change archetypal journey upon the Flat Arc character's story—but with a supporting character enacting the actual journey. The Flat archetypal protagonist will still be the primary actor within the conflict (which is ultimately how we define which character is the protagonist). But his or her actions and adherence to the thematic Truth will allow other characters to move forward in their own life journeys. Depending on the specifics of the story, the supporting character's Change Arc may feature prominently *or* may appear only in a subplot.

WRITING ARCHETYPAL CHARACTER ARCS | 205

We can see how this works perhaps most obviously in the relationship between the Hero and the Mentor. The Flat Mentor archetype is an easily recognizable Impact Character within the classical Hero's Journey. But if we flip the script, the Mentor becomes the protagonist, and the Hero becomes a supporting character. Unlike a Hero Arc, in which the Mentor almost always dies to facilitate a sensible reason for the immature Hero to be the one to end the conflict, a Mentor story often pits the Hero and the Mentor against differing and more "age-appropriate" antagonists.

A perfect example of this can be found in *The Lord of the Rings*, in which the character Gandalf is arguably the story's protagonist. Certainly, he displays agency and centrality to the conflict throughout. He focuses on the supernatural antagonists that only he can confront, while the Heroes, Queens, and Kings are inspired by his example to fight their own battles and enact their own Change Arcs.

How the Shadow Archetypes Relate to the Flat Archetypes

None of the six Flat archetypes we will be discussing in this section are naturally negative. However, the twelve shadow archetypes we explored in the previous section are often relatively static. The passive negative archetypes in particular tend to remain stuck in their own fear and complacency. These characters can be used as protagonists or antagonists within Negative Flat Arcs, in which the protagonist influences supporting characters for the *worse*.

However, in stories with *positive* Flat Arc protagonists, the shadow archetypes are more likely to show up either as antagonists or as the supporting characters who will be inspired to undertake positive journeys thanks to the protagonist's influence.

Usually, any negative archetypes within a Flat Arc story will be those from arcs that preceded the protagonist's. For example, if the protagonist is a Parent (the flat or resting form of the Queen), then she is most likely to interact with the negative archetypes of Damsel/Vixen, Coward/Bully, or Snow Queen/Sorceress. This is because these "younger" archetypes are the only ones she is equipped to help or defeat at this stage of her own growth. Should she be challenged by a later negative archetype—such as the Puppet/Tyrant—she would need to advance out of the Parent archetype and change into a full-blown Queen Arc.

A Flat Arc story will be about a character who understands something important that the rest of the story world does not. It is a story about this character using this understanding to advance and benefit the current story world.

***

Flat Arc stories are not mythic journeys in the same way as the six foundational life arc archetypes. Although Flat Arc stories show supporting characters undergoing transformative arcs, Flat Arcs themselves are more varied and episodic than the six archetypal Positive Change character arcs. This is because there are many *types* of stories that can be told about a Child or a Ruler or an Elder. Indeed, many people spend years, or even decades, within the same Flat archetype before life confronts them with new challenges that demand they journey on into the subsequent life arc.

As such, I am not offering a "mythic beat sheet" for the Flat archetypes in the same way as I did for the positive archetypes. Over the course of the next six chapters, we will be diving into the foundational aspects of these interstitial Flat archetypes and looking at how you can recreate these important archetypes within your own stories.

"When we are children we
seldom think of the future.
This innocence leaves us free
to enjoy ourselves as few adults can.
The day we fret about the future is the day
we leave our childhood behind."
—Patrick Rothfuss

16

THE CHILD

IN MANY WAYS, the Child is hardly a Flat or unchanging archetype at all. Even though we often perceive and remember childhood as a chapter in which everything remained the same (until suddenly it didn't), the years before puberty are, of course, some of the most rapidly transformational of any part of our lives. And yet for all children there is a definitive sameness to this period of life. No matter our individual personalities or family circumstances, we are all *children*—innocents, blank slates. More than that, we are free from the responsibility of growth that arrives with burgeoning adolescence and the onset of the Maiden Arc.

At first glance, the Child archetype may seem lacking in the necessary Flat Arc ability to transform the story world or supporting characters. However, I think any adult who has had a child enter his or her life will attest that few grown-ups are as utterly transformative and growth-inducing as are children!

More than that, the Child is often a surprisingly wise archetype. If we recognize that story structure always comes full circle, we can see how the final character arc of the life cycle—the enlightened Mage—is in many ways a fulfilled *return* to the Child's deep connection to and instinctive understanding of life.

In her book *Awakening the Heroes Within: Twelve Archetypes to Help Us Find Ourselves and Transform Our World*, Carol S. Pearson opens her cycle of archetypes with what she calls the Innocent and ends (even after her Magician) with the Fool—which she also calls the Wise Innocent and which she considers the highest of all the archetypes. She speaks of this end-of-life return to the beginning in a way that highlights many of the inherent if unconscious attributes of the Child archetype.

If the Mage's full-circle epiphany ends the life arcs, then it is the Child at the beginning who represents all this capacity for joy, innocence, trust, and resilience—but from a place of no power and no experience. As such, the Child is necessarily an archetype of deep vulnerability.

A fortunate Child will be protected from dangers until adolescence finally demands an opening of the eyes and an embarkation upon the initiatory journey of the Maiden Arc. But even Children who are not forced to precipitously undertake their first Change Arc will still encounter many opportunities for adventures and discovery, particularly as they witness and influence the growth of supporting characters around them.

THE CHILD ARCHETYPE: UNTAPPED POTENTIAL

Previous Arc: [None]
Subsequent Positive Arc: Maiden
Subsequent Negative Archetypes: Damsel (passive); Vixen (aggressive)

The Maiden Arc is traditionally the "Young Adult" time of a person's life—beginning as early as puberty but often not fully culminating until the mid to late teens. Therefore, the earlier Child archetype is one we generally find represented by characters younger than thirteen or so.

Their stories are often full of magic and nostalgia. Even if the plot itself revolves around adults in difficult or even dark circumstances, the story is poignantly represented through the limited understanding of the Child protagonist. Classics such as *Anne of Green Gables* and *To Kill a Mockingbird* show us adult worlds through the eyes of Child protagonists. Even when heavy subjects are at play (i.e., problematic foster systems and

WRITING ARCHETYPAL CHARACTER ARCS | 213

racial injustice), the stories themselves are surprisingly whimsical.

Despite whatever difficulties these Child protagonists may have so far endured in their lives, they have yet maintained their innocence. They are yet "one" with society's protective figures, un-individuated from those whom they trust (or at least hope) will care for their needs. They haven't yet cultivated the cynicism or irony of someone who has learned what the world is really about—namely, taking responsibility for one's self. *Anne of Green Gables* is an obvious (and perhaps extreme) example of a Child protagonist who starts the story having undergone severe neglect and even abuse, and yet who miraculously and tenaciously clings to her childish wonder of a world that she persists in believing is glorious, romantic, and even magical.

The Child is an archetype of untapped potential. We all know this character will grow up, will hit puberty, will be confronted with the Maiden's challenges of initiating. The innocence will be shaken and fade for at least a time. But within the Child archetype, we also find the promise of what can be reclaimed if this character is eventually able to complete the cycle of life arcs.

THE CHILD'S NORMAL WORLD

The Normal World in which the Child begins the story is the Home. It is a comparatively small place, bounded by the rules, protection, and love of a Parent or other protective figure. Already we see where later archetypes might show up (the Parent/Queen as well as perhaps older siblings in the guise of Maiden or Hero).

Within this world, the Child has a surprising amount of freedom. Unlike later archetypes, the Child has few responsibilities imposed either from without or from within. The Child is free to roam, to play, and to discover. Usually, it is this propensity for discovery that creates the dilemmas and opportunities of the story's plot.

Many an episodic children's series (such as one of my childhood favorites, *Trixie Belden*) centers around the protagonist's incorrigible curiosity and the mysteries they keep sniffing out, book after book. Particularly in stories aimed at a child audience, these protagonists never change much, never grow up. But their innocence in "not knowing any better" often leads them to insights the adults around them would never have noticed.

Some stories feature a Normal World that is not safe and static, but that is changing right around the Child protagonist, even though the Child doesn't yet notice. The Child has no idea life is about to forever change (and probably launch a Maiden Arc). Rather, the character romps through the last halcyon adventures of a dying age, such as in Rob Reiner's classic film *Stand by Me*, set in the 1950s.

The Child's Relationship to the Thematic Truth

Although the Child will likely learn many things, he or she will not fundamentally change except perhaps at the very end of the story with the foreshadowing of the Maiden Arc. Instead, as with all Flat Arc characters, the Child will (probably unwittingly) convey a thematic Truth to at least one supporting character, who will change as a result. Depending on how prominent the role is, the supporting character may or may not undergo a fully developed archetypal journey.

Because the Child has not, in fact, *learned* any archetypal Truths at this point in his or her young life, the thematic Truths in these stories tend to focus around the perennial themes and gifts of childhood: innocence, joy, love, presence, playfulness, loyalty, etc. The naïvety and purity of the Child allows the character to believe in the uncorrupted virtues that many adults struggle with and/or mourn for the rest of their lives.

How the Child Creates Change in Supporting Characters

Unlike other Flat archetypes, the Child has not yet personally gleaned Truths that can be shared with younger characters. All of the characters will either be fellow Children at the same level of innocence or older characters who are much farther along the archetypal journey of growth.

And yet the Child's natural wisdom still has the ability to profoundly impact the Change Arcs of supporting characters. Even if the supporting characters resist the change inspired by the Child, the audience will still understand the profundity of the Child's simplicity.

The Child has the opportunity to offer a sort of "redemption" or return to innocence to older, more hardened supporting characters. We can see this in *Anne of Green Gables*, in which the buoyant orphan Anne revitalizes the lonely and hardened older couple with whom she comes to live, and in *Oliver Twist*, in which Oliver (another orphan) inspires compassion and ultimately fatal virtue in the prostitute Nancy who tries to help him escape London's criminal underworld.

Types of Stories That Feature a Child Protagonist

Even more than with most Flat Arc archetypes, the possibilities are particularly vast for the type of story that features a Child protagonist. The story might be fun and funny or dark and dangerous. It can be about the relationship between the Child and other Children, or about the Child and any of the adult archetypes. It may be a story of redemption for an adult character, or it may be a story about a family overcoming adversity. It can be set in any time or place and can be framed within any genre. It can be written for children or for adults.

Cozy mysteries and memoir-like adventures are popular and fun for Child characters. But serious social commentaries such as *To Kill a Mockingbird* can be all the more powerful for their atypical narrator/main character.

In many ways, the "untapped potential" of the Child archetype makes it one of the most versatile of all the Flat archetypes. In fact, writing a Child character can invite us back into the uncensored creative options of this foundational period in all our lives.

EXAMPLES OF THE CHILD

Examples of the Child archetype include the following.
- Scout Finch in *To Kill a Mockingbird*
- Tom Sawyer in *Tom Sawyer*
- Anne Shirley in *Anne of Green Gables*
- Oliver Twist in *Oliver Twist*
- Johnny Dorset in "The Ransom of Red Chief"
- Nat Cooper in *Forever Young*
- Trixie Belden in *Trixie Belden*
- Gordie LaChance in *Stand by Me*
- Jane and Michael Banks in *Mary Poppins*
- Pollyanna Whittier in *Pollyanna*
- Violet, Klaus, and Sunny Baudelaire in *A Series of Unfortunate Events*
- Lex and Timmy Murphy in *Jurassic Park*

"...the role of the artist is exactly the same as
the role of the lover. If I love you,
I have to make you conscious
of the things you don't see."
—James Baldwin

17

The Lover

THE LOVER ARCHETYPE is inherent and even integral within the human life cycle. Although it is a deeply nuanced archetype that evolves with us for most of our lives—and shows up in many guises—it is particularly foundational to the First Act of life, when it emerges in response to the coming-of-age lessons of the Maiden Arc.

The archetypal Lover, as I will be discussing it here, is not simply a person who falls in love. Obviously, falling in love can happen at any stage of one's life and in correlation to any of the progressive archetypal character arcs. Specifically, the Lover as a Flat archetype within this particular system of archetypes refers to first love or young love. It is the period of awakened love and sexuality in which a character is just beginning to explore what it might mean to no longer be "one" with the tribe, but simply "one" with another "one."

This is not a mature love. It is the intense, wonderful, passionate, exploratory, sometimes frightening first love of the young adult. Although it signifies growth, it is also an ironically destructive force, since it signifies the means and the route by which the youth finds a path away from the necessary "mother love" of the parents, from whom he or she has only so recently begun to individuate, and into the possibility of supportive love and union with another individuated person.

As the resting period between the crucibles of the Maiden and the Hero Arcs, the Lover also represents the foundation the Hero will need in order to move forward into his all-important quest. As discussed in Chapter 3, the Hero Arc completes the youthful initiations of life's First Act and is ultimately about learning to submit one's personal power to a worthy love.

Although often represented as such, the love of the Hero is not specifically a romantic love. Rather, it is a love that allows the mature adult to reintegrate with the tribe from which he has now successfully individuated. His explorations of love both prior to and during his transformative arc rest upon the Lover archetype, which knits together the journeys of the Maiden and the Hero.

Because the Lover has so far completed only one arc (the Maiden), the love experienced in this period is still unformed, possessive, immature, and often unindividuated. It is the teenage love eulogized in so many pop songs. The love that will be experienced later in the Hero Arc will then be the maturing of this potential into a deeper, richer, more developed love—one that can give without giving away one's self.

THE LOVER ARCHETYPE: EMPOWERED YOUTH

Previous Arc: Maiden
Subsequent Positive Arc: Hero
Subsequent Possible Negative Archetypes: Coward (passive); Bully (aggressive)

There is a reason Young Adult romance is so popular. At hardly any other time in life are you so consistently likely to experience the overwhelming intensity of emotion that is available when you are young enough to be in love but not yet fully emerged into the adult you will become. Young love is a fusion, not always completely centered or healthy, but always transformative.

What is important about placing the Lover archetype between the Maiden and the Hero Arcs is the emphasis upon the character's newly growing agency, which is closely linked to

WRITING ARCHETYPAL CHARACTER ARCS | 223

burgeoning sexuality. The previous Maiden Arc focuses upon an awakening from childhood into adulthood. That arc ends with the character beginning to step into adult power, and that power is very likely to be expressed, openly or otherwise, via the character's budding pursuit of romance.

Like the Child archetype before it, the Lover archetype clearly represents a volcano of transformation. But as discussed here, the Lover *is* a Flat archetype. This is not because falling in love, especially for the first time, does not create massive transformation within a person. Rather, it is because the actual change that is linked to growing into and out of this archetype is addressed in the previous Maiden Arc and subsequent Hero Arc.

THE LOVER'S NORMAL WORLD

The Lover is a character who has completed the previous Maiden Arc. The archetype can be represented by a person of any age, but chronologically within the cycle, the character is still quite young—mid to late teens. As shown in so many YA stories, this is a character who is perhaps just finishing up high school (and preparing for the Hero's quest that will follow). The character senses the changes gathering on the horizon, but does not yet need to fully face them.

Having gained the right and ability to move beyond the walls of the family home in the Maiden Arc, the Lover's Normal World is now represented by the slightly larger confines of the village. The character's world has broadened beyond simply that of parents and siblings. Friends, teachers, and employers are now relationships he or she must navigate on the way to finding a grown-up role amongst the tribe.

The Lover still shares quite a bit in common with the Child, but the Child's foundational innocence is now gone. The Lover now knows the world is *not* unchanging, and he or she is not unchanging in it. There is now a great deal of uncertainty in the world of which the character was not previously aware. The character is no longer completely at ease within this world, and as a result, the world itself will be challenged to change itself to accommodate this character—who is suddenly no longer a predictable Child.

The Lover's Relationship to the Thematic Truth

What Truth has a character so young and unsteady as the Lover to communicate to supporting characters? Unlike the Child, who in some ways represents "all" potential truths simply because the Child does not yet have any *personal* truths, the Lover now has at least one Truth—gained from the transformation of the Maiden Arc. The essence of that Truth is "personal sovereignty is necessary for growth and survival."

The Lover is such a young character that he or she is unlikely to be particularly articulate about this Truth. This character's ability to create transformational change in others is far less about "telling" them anything and much more about the catalyzing influence of the youthful person's very existence. The young flame burns brightly, and it acts as both effortless inspiration to those who would follow and unspoken reminder to those who have gone before.

How the Lover Creates Change in Supporting Characters

In discussing the Lover here, we are discussing the interstitial period when a character has individuated enough to fall in love but has not yet been asked to fully grapple with the ramifications of the great life change that will occur in the Hero Arc. Instead, the Lover is a static character who is able to influence change upon others. Having undergone the Maiden Arc, this character already knows something many of his or her peers will not yet have learned (and, indeed, something many adults have either never fully integrated or somewhat forgotten).

As with all the Flat archetypes, the Lover is most likely to encourage change in those characters who are "behind" within the cycle. At this point, that means the characters most likely

WRITING ARCHETYPAL CHARACTER ARCS | 225

to be changed by a Lover protagonist are those who are on the Maiden Arc themselves.

Most obviously, the Lover is likely to encourage a transformation in the very person he or she loves. Indeed, falling in love for the first time can be the transformational spark that sets off the Maiden Arc. It is certainly possible (and common) for two young characters to be concurrently taking the Maiden Arc. However, it is also possible that a Lover character, who has already arced, is the one catalyzing transformation for the other person. Indeed, the ability to choose wisely and well *whom* to love is one of the great challenges of this individuation period.

Types of Stories That Feature a Lover Protagonist

The Lover most obviously appears in love stories—usually coming-of-age love stories. Sometimes these stories offer happy endings; just as often, and perhaps more realistically, they end tragically with the realization that however formative this early love affair, it cannot last into the next journey.

However, Lover stories don't absolutely have to be about a protagonist who falls in love with another person. What is important in utilizing this archetype is recognizing it as the interstitial period between the transformations of Maiden and Hero. Ultimately, what the Lover represents is discovery. In *Sacred Contracts*, Caroline Myss speaks of the Lover archetype (which she references more broadly and does not confine to this early period of life) as being defined by "passion" and "devotion":

> This archetype appears not only in those who are romantically inclined, but also in anyone who exhibits great passion and devotion. One can be a Lover of art, music, gardening, Persian carpets, nature, or needlepoint. The key is having a sense of unbridled and exaggerated affection and appreciation of someone or something that influences the organization of your life and environment.

We can find this in many coming-of-age stories which simultaneously develop the Lover character's young romances alongside an exploration of some passion or talent, such as that of the Pre-Raphaelite painters of the 19th-century as portrayed in the BBC's (not particularly historical or flattering) miniseries *Desperate Romantics*.

What defines a Lover story (in comparison to a Maiden or Hero story) is its somewhat episodic nature. Regardless of whatever joy or sorrow the protagonist may experience, and regardless how drastically the supporting characters may evolve, the story's symbolic setting will not change. The Maiden Arc sees the protagonist move, symbolically, from home to village, and the Hero Arc sees the protagonist move from village to kingdom. But the Lover remains in the village throughout. The Hero Arc will beckon later on.

EXAMPLES OF THE LOVER

Examples of the Lover archetype include the following.

- Everybody in *Sense & Sensibility*
- Everybody in *Desperate Romantics*
- Tom in *500 Days of Summer*
- Westley and Buttercup in *The Princess Bride*
- Augustus Waters in *The Fault in Our Stars*
- Tony and Maria in *West Side Story*
- Arwen in *The Lord of the Rings*
- Elsa Dutton in *1883*

"In a world that changes rapidly,
it is a rare set of parents who actually can
groom the next generation
for what is to come."
—Carol S. Pearson

18

The Parent

WHEN WE THINK of archetypal characters, the Parent probably isn't the first to come to mind. Despite the fact that becoming and being a parent is one of the most obvious initiations in our modern lives, we don't often think of the Parent with the same enthusiasm as we do the Hero. And yet the two are intrinsically linked.

The Parent is the Flat or resting archetype that follows or results from what is currently our most iconic character arc—the Hero's Journey. In some ways, as with all archetypes, this is merely a symbolic evolution, since not all Heroes fresh from their quests will literally settle down to start families. But not only is the Parent historically the next obvious step for the Hero, this archetype is also a deeply symbolic transitional period between the First Act of a character's life and the Second Act.

Remember, the First Act of the life cycle of archetypal character arcs represents approximately the first thirty years of the human life, during which the primary transformation struggles of the Maiden and Hero Arcs are defined by the challenges of Relationship With Self. Successful completion of the Hero Arc signifies that the character has been able to achieve both individuation from the tribe as a child and reintegration back into it as an adult.

Now, as the Parent, the character represents the fulcrum of the turning point into the challenges of the Second Act, during which the primary transformation struggles of the Queen and King Arcs will be defined by the challenges of Relationship With Others—and particularly the power dynamics of relating to younger people.

The Parent's "rest" (and I know all parents are laughing at the word!) before the next transformation of the Queen Arc signifies a period in which the character can regroup after the travails and victories of the now completed Hero's quest. In essence, the character is a soldier returned from war who may now enjoy a hard-won and justly deserved peace.

More than that, as a Flat archetype, the Parent has the opportunity to bless the Kingdom to which he or she has returned. The character is now an adult with a good deal of important life experience. Whether the character uses this experience to teach and rear actual children or more symbolically in simply contributing to the health of the larger community, the result will be the opportunity for other characters to learn from the Parent's hard-won thematic truths.

THE PARENT ARCHETYPE: THE HERO AT HOME

Previous Arc: Hero
Subsequent Positive Arc: Queen
Subsequent Possible Negative Archetypes: Snow Queen (passive); Sorceress (aggressive)

It has become something of a cliché that the Hero's Journey should end with the protagonist "getting the girl and riding into the sunset." Usual complaints aside, this in fact refers to something of deep symbolic import. Specifically, what is being dramatized is the Hero's return to and reintegration into the community, not just as the youth he was before, but as someone ready to form a union with another person and perhaps begin raising and teaching the next generation.

The central challenge of the Hero Arc is that of submitting his power to a "love worth fighting for." Within the Hero Arc

WRITING ARCHETYPAL CHARACTER ARCS | 233

itself, it is possible (although not required) that this love be romantic. By the time the Hero has returned to the Kingdom to become the Parent, that love will extend to encompass a much larger family to which the character is now willingly responsible.

In many ways, the Parent represents the mysterious "happily ever after" that classically ends so many Hero stories (and, again, I know actual parents may be snickering!). It is a time when the harvest of the character's life is ripe. Even if circumstances are not literally perfect in the external world (e.g., the character works long hours in or out of the home to care for the family), they are stable. The character is primarily content with the status quo. Any personal changes that are yet to occur will take place later in the subsequent Queen Arc. For now "war is over," and life seems to be going exactly as expected.

THE PARENT'S NORMAL WORLD

After the questing of the Hero Arc, the Parent has returned home once more. However, it can be helpful to realize that the village that comprised the Normal World at the beginning of the Hero Arc has, at least from the character's perspective, broadened into a larger kingdom. Having seen the world during the quest, the character understands the world is a larger, more interconnected place than was obvious in the First Act arcs.

More specifically, however, the Parent's Normal World can be thought of as "the hearth," since the primary focus is on what is happening in the character's own home rather than "out there" in the larger world. The primary focus within this interstitial period is that of nurturing others, loving them, raising them, teaching them, and helping them grow.

This is, of course, where we see the cycle start to repeat. Both the Child archetype and the Maiden archetype began with a young person facing the challenges of separating from the Parent and the hearth. Now, that Child has become the very Parent from whom the next generation will eventually have to individuate as well. Indeed, the next challenge for the Parent, in the subsequent Queen Arc, will be that of *letting* the Maidens individuate.

For now, however, this challenge remains in the future, as the Children are yet too young and dependent. At this stage, it is vital that the responsible Parent provide the love and security that will give the Children a strong foundation from which to begin their own arcs.

The Parent's Relationship to the Thematic Truth

Although the Parent, like all the Flat archetypes, does not represent transformation, it *does* represent a period of great valor. More than ever, the Parent represents a character who now bears great responsibilities for the well-being of others. True Parents (who do not devolve into the negative counter-archetypes) will prove themselves steady in the face of trial and temptation.

The true Parent is able to act as a positive and stable force within the world thanks to the thematic Truths learned in the previous arcs, and especially the immediately previous arc of the Hero. That Truth may be thought of as simply, "All my actions affect those I love." By completing the Hero Arc, the Parent has already proved his or her ability to sacrifice out of love. Now that sacrifice continues in a more prosaic (but no less poignant) way. It is via the daily affirmation of this heroic Truth that the Parent is able to enact tremendous change within the lives of supporting characters.

How the Parent Creates Change in Supporting Characters

Most obviously, the Parent will parent his or her own children. But the relationship can, of course, also be symbolic. The Parent may mentor children or young people who are not related, or may even act the parental role toward chronological peers. What is important is simply that the "children" are characters who have not yet reached the same level of initiation as the Parent.

WRITING ARCHETYPAL CHARACTER ARCS | 235

Although the Parent can influence change for any younger archetype, he or she is most likely to enact an important formative relationship with the Maiden. The Parent/Maiden dynamic is extremely important, since the Maiden Arc represents an individual's first and most important struggle against the Parent. This almost always creates a tremendous challenge not just for the Maiden who is beginning to individuate, but for the Parent as well. Parents who understand the lessons of the previous arcs can consciously allow and even guide a young Maiden in separating from them.

To the degree the Parent fails in representing the thematic Truth to the Maiden (or any other character), he or she risks becoming the antagonist in that supporting character's own story, as we've seen via the Maiden's symbolic antagonists of Too-Good Mother, Naïve Father, and even Predator (which will be discussed in more depth in Chapter 23).

Types of Stories That Feature a Parent Protagonist

The Parent most obviously shows up in stories of family drama or comedy. Sometimes these stories are explicitly about the trials of being a parent, such as in Steve Martin's comedy *Parenthood*. Or the story could be about the coming-of-age of a Maiden but shown through the perspective of the Parent.

Stories in which a Parent takes on the system to defend a child in some way are widespread. It's also common to see the Parent represented by a teacher character who acts positively within the lives of students, even or especially if the students are not receiving proper parenting at home. Parent protagonists can also be seen in stories that focus less on actual parenting and more on the struggles of providing for one's family.

What is central to all these stories is the specific relationship dynamic of a character who provides some sort of care and guidance for at least one younger or more vulnerable character.

EXAMPLES OF THE PARENT

Examples of the Parent archetype include the following.

- Mrs. Weasley in *Harry Potter and the Philosopher's Stone* (among others)
- M'Lynn Eatenton in *Steel Magnolias*
- Kay Miniver in *Mrs. Miniver*
- Marmee March in *Little Women*
- Hans and Rosa Hubermann in *The Book Thief*
- Andy Taylor in *The Andy Griffith Show*
- The Buckman siblings in *Parenthood*

"If your actions inspire others to dream more, learn more, do more and become more, you are a leader."
—John Quincy Adams

19

THE RULER

THE RULER REPRESENTS the Flat or resting archetype that bridges the Queen's rise to power and the King's eventual surrender of that same power. As such, the Ruler represents the potential period in a person's life in which he or she is in a position of leadership.

This Ruler might be a literal head of state—queen, king, president, prime minister, etc. Or the Ruler might be a CEO, general, admiral, lead scientist, patriarch or matriarch, captain of a ship, sheriff, etc. What is important to this archetype (and what distinguishes it from the previous Flat archetype of Parent) is that the Ruler is not just "in charge" in some limited capacity but is the undisputed authority within his or her sphere of influence.

The Ruler is not merely the loving guide represented by the Parent, although in a healthy Ruler character, the Parent will of course have been incorporated into this more advanced archetype. The Ruler is someone who has learned the hard lessons of the Queen's rise to power and now understands that the primary challenge of true leadership is that of creating order. A good Ruler understands mercy, but will err toward justice. As a result, the Kingdom runs smoothly and successfully (or at least until the dawn of the subsequent King Arc signals it is time for the crown to be passed on).

From a real-world perspective, the Ruler is one of the most powerful of all archetypes. Perhaps literally or perhaps symbolically within the sphere of any specific story's smaller "Kingdom," the Ruler's word is law. The decisions made by such a character have vast reach and will affect the lives of all characters living within the Kingdom, both the younger and, likely, the older archetypes as well. Right away, we can see what a powerful protagonist the Ruler makes within a Flat Arc, in which the protagonist does not change but instead enacts and offers the opportunity for change to the supporting characters.

The Ruler Archetype: True Sovereignty

Previous Arc: Queen
Subsequent Positive Arc: King
Subsequent Possible Negative Archetypes: Puppet (passive); Tyrant (aggressive)

The Ruler represents the height of a person's power potential. This archetype rests at the very center of the entire life cycle. It is the true Midpoint between the Second Act arcs of Queen and King. As such, the Ruler is a character who has long since overcome the primary challenges of mastering the inner world (challenges which were conquered in the young Maiden and Hero Arcs), but has also gained a significant amount of control over the outer world (thanks to the Queen Arc). Indeed, it is because of the Ruler's inner-world control that he or she is able to bring similar order and blessing to the outer Kingdom. The Ruler is able to master the Kingdom precisely because he or she has first mastered the self.

We can see this validated if we return to the symbolism of the classical Hero's Journey, in which the young Hero is often called on his quest because the King/Ruler is sick, resulting in a related sickness upon the entire Kingdom. In short: healthy Ruler = healthy Kingdom. (We'll discuss the archetypal antagonist of the "Sick King" further in Chapter 24.)

A Ruler who can bless the Kingdom with health is someone who has achieved true sovereignty. A worthy leader is a person who has first mastered or gained sovereignty over himself. Indeed, the hallmark of a negative Ruler is disrespect for either one's own personal sovereignty (the Puppet) or that of others (the Tyrant).

THE RULER'S NORMAL WORLD

Aptly, the Ruler's Normal World may be viewed symbolically as a Kingdom. However, it is not necessary for the character to literally rule over a nation. Whatever his or her realm of influence, *that* is the story's Kingdom.

The protagonist does not need to be wealthy or even to rule over a great number of "subjects." Whatever his sphere of influence, the Ruler has reached the top—and he's happy there. If his Kingdom is Jeff Bridges's floating school for troubled boys in *White Squall*, then he is content to rule that Kingdom. He is not ambitious. Although he will always be trying to better the lot of his subjects, he is not trying to advance his own position because, archetypally, he is already at the top.

(In case you were wondering, we can know the Jeff Bridges character is primarily a Ruler archetype instead of a Parent archetype because his focus is not on loving the boys in his charge but rather on helping them become responsible citizens by imposing order upon them. He's not protecting them as Children, but demanding they carry their weight as "citizens" within their little floating Kingdom.)

The Kingdom will be a self-contained unit with defined borders. Rulers are not the rulers of *everything* (unless, of course, they are). Rather, they are finite sovereigns of finite realms with finite borders. As such, they will recognize and make treaties with other Rulers of other realms.

Whatever the story's specific Kingdom, it will be a space in which the Ruler can work to effectively impose order and productivity. To whatever degree possible, the Ruler will work to better the lot of the Kingdom's subjects and keep the system running smoothly.

The Ruler's Relationship to the Thematic Truth

The Ruler is a very advanced archetype—one that only a few people truly embody. By this point in the life cycle, the Ruler has successfully learned and integrated many Truths—most recently the Queen Arc's "only wise leadership and trust in those I love can protect them and allow us all to grow." But the very fact that this character is a Ruler—and presumably a pretty good one—means there are many thematic Truths available to be handed down to the Kingdom.

This is a character who is not just brave, smart, and caring, but a character who has integrated all the previous arcs' lessons into a deeply practical wisdom. Even when the Ruler makes mistakes, this is still a character who has much to offer everyone else.

How the Ruler Creates Change in Supporting Characters

A good Ruler is most likely to interact with the younger Heroes, initiating them on their quests into adulthood. As with all the older archetypes, the Ruler offers a vital transaction within the life-arc cycle. This transaction represents the ability of the mature archetypes to initiate the younger archetypes in their own journeys.

A good Ruler may also work to transform an upcoming Queen. This might seem surprising at first glance, since the Queen Arc is usually about supplanting a previously *unworthy* King. But in reality, the Queen's transition into leadership need not be so dramatic. If she is fortunate enough to succeed a good Ruler, that Ruler will not stand in the way of her rise. When it is time for him to take his own King Arc and step down from the throne, he will pass on the crown to a worthy successor whom he has himself blessed and trained up.

WRITING ARCHETYPAL CHARACTER ARCS | 245

Types of Stories That Feature a Ruler Protagonist

Certain stories about teachers are often Ruler stories (again, those that focus more on imposing healthy order and maturing their students into adulthood, rather than nurturing the students' Child capacities). War stories, such as *Band of Brothers* and the Captain America stories in the Marvel Cinematic Universe, which focus on the burden of command, can feature Rulers.

And, of course, Ruler characters are often just that—rulers of countries, kingdoms, villages, galaxies, etc. Flat Arc stories about monarchs and presidents are almost always stories about Rulers (unless, of course, they are stories about Puppets or Tyrants).

Usually, a Ruler story will feature strong subplots about the arcs of the younger characters who are influenced by the Ruler protagonist. If the story is truly a Flat Arc that features a Ruler protagonist (versus a Change Arc in which the protagonist is a younger archetype and the Ruler is instead a supporting Impact Character), the Ruler will still be presented as the character with the most agency at all of the important structural beats.

Examples of the Ruler

Examples of the Ruler archetype include the following.

- Mr. Knightley in *Emma*
- Leia Organa in *Star Wars*
- Jack Aubrey in the Aubrey/Maturin series
- Steve Rogers in the Marvel Cinematic Universe
- Furiosa in *Mad Max: Fury Road*
- Skipper Sheldon in *White Squall*
- Dick Winters in *Band of Brothers*
- Sister Julienne in *Call the Midwife*
- Coach Norman Dale in *Hoosiers*
- Andrew Shepherd in *American President*

"I believe in old age; to work and to grow old:
this is what life expects of us.
And then one day to be old and still be quite far
from understanding everything—
no, but to begin, but to love, but to suspect,
but to be connected to what is remote
and inexpressible, all the way up into the stars."
—Rainer Maria Rilke

20

THE ELDER

WITHIN A POSITIVE Change Arc, an Impact Character is the character who represents the thematic Truth and its potential to "impact" and change the protagonist. However, within a Flat Arc, the protagonist *is* the Impact Character. As we delve into the Flat archetypes of the life cycle's Third Act, we begin to see more and more definitely just how impactful the archetypes of old age can be.

Indeed, we are most familiar with the Flat archetypes of Elder and Mentor for the very reason that they commonly appear in younger Change Arcs as important Impact Characters. We are most likely to recognize the Mentor as a staple within the Hero's Journey, but the preceding Elder archetype is no less viable or important, even though it may be a bit more prosaic.

The Elder is the resting archetype that lives between the tremendously transformative Change Arcs of the King—which concluded the cycle's Second Act as the final adult arc—and the Crone—which as the first of the two old-age archetypes in the Third Act signifies the character's graduation into true elderhood. While the subsequent Flat archetype of Mentor may be more proactive in guiding the young up-and-coming protagonists into the next generational cycle, the Elder is no less influential in providing crucial guidance and catalyzing important change in surrounding characters.

The Elder: Making Peace With Death

Previous Arc: King
Subsequent Arc: Crone
Subsequent Possible Negative Archetypes: Hermit (passive); Witch (active)

Essentially, the Elder is the resting form of the Crone. As such, this character is in a state of integration after the tremendous trials and sacrifices of the previous King Arc, which ended with a self-sacrificial retreat into the "elder realm."

We can clearly see the Elder in the beginning of the Crone's First Act when the Elder is yet undecided about whether to answer the next Call to Adventure and embark upon a further transformation. In this period, and the entire resting stage prior to it, the Crone can be seen to have retreated from the world.

Symbolically, the Elder lives apart from the Kingdom, in a secluded hut in the woods. More prosaically, this is a character who has retired from the hustle-bustle of commercial, political, or social concerns. He or she is no longer at the center of the whirling challenges of power and relationship. The character may be withered, perhaps even physically infirm or limited.

Assuming this character has successfully and willingly completed the previous King Arc, this current state is one to which he or she is at least partially reconciled. It is, however, totally possible for a character to simply be dumped into this phase by the inevitable encroachment of old age. Either way, the character is understandably in a phase of grief, recovery, and integration.

As the subsequent Change Arcs of Crone and Mage ripely prove, there is within this character, perhaps not so surprisingly, what Clarissa Pinkola Estés refers to as the "fecundity" of "black soil glittering with mica, black hairy roots, and all the life that has gone before."

This deep black soil is the treasure of a life's work. However altered the Elder's circumstances—from palace to hut—this is a character who has lived a full and good life. This is a character

WRITING ARCHETYPAL CHARACTER ARCS | 251

who has seen and met many challenges and, if a true Elder, has overcome those challenges with grace, courage, and wisdom.

In short, this is a character with a lot to teach just about everyone else. In no small part, it is in this teaching—this ability to impact the coming generation—that the Elder will find personal healing and the strength to embark on the tremendous Change Arcs of the Third Act.

THE ELDER'S NORMAL WORLD

At first glance, we might think we see the Elder in the symbolism of the scary old woman, such as the Baba Yaga of the Eastern European tales, who lives in a hut deep in the woods and hangs dead cats and other horrors outside her house. The children dare each other to look through her window, convincing themselves she is a witch. She may play along, in part as jest, in part as unspoken test, and in part because she's not so sure she wouldn't just rather be alone.

We see this in many stories about the brave young person—the budding Maiden—who dares to keep coming back to visit the grumpy oldster, as in Shirley MacLaine's *The Last Word* and Bill Murray's *St. Vincent*, among many others.

It isn't strictly necessary that the Elder live alone or even apart from society. This is merely a symbolic representation of how the Third Act of life is separated from the previous two acts in definite if sometimes vague ways. It is totally possible that the Elder character lives *with* the children or grandchildren or other relatives.

A good example is found in Truman Capote's autobiographical stories, such as "A Christmas Memory," about his childhood friendship with an elderly cousin while both were living with and dependent upon other "less understanding" relatives. Even though the cousin isn't stereotypically grumpy, she is clearly removed from the bustle of "grown-up life," just as she has also clearly not yet taken her next transformation into the profound understanding that comes with the subsequent Crone Arc.

If you are to tell a Flat Arc story about an Elder, what is important is that the character's self-imposed isolation or separation is breached in some way. Other characters, after all, have to get in, in order to be transformed by the Elder's wisdom. (If the story is about an older protagonist on a lonely quest—such as in David Guterson's novel *East of the Mountains*—then it is probably not an Elder's Flat Arc, but rather a Crone's Change Arc.)

THE ELDER'S RELATIONSHIP TO THE THEMATIC TRUTH

Why does the Elder have different or *more* thematic Truths to teach than the previous Flat archetypes of Parent and Ruler? Although, obviously, the Elder has lived longer and inevitably picked up a few more clues along the way, the real difference is that the Truths of the Third Act are of a different caliber than those of the previous two acts, however related.

Having just completed the King Arc, the Elder has most recently assimilated a Truth that might be phrased as: "Spiritual strength and physical strength are not always the same. Indeed, sometimes one must be willing to sacrifice the latter for the former."

Whatever thematic Truth is presented in an Elder story will largely depend on whatever the younger Change Arc supporting character needs to learn. At this point, the Elder has done it all (or almost all), at least archetypally speaking. Whatever practical or relational problem the younger character is struggling with will be one the Elder knows the answer to, if only by dint of time and experience. Even in stories such as *St. Vincent*, in which the character has clearly *not* aced all his previous arcs and is in many ways a seeming failure, he still knows what the young Change Arc character needs in order to advance.

HOW THE ELDER CREATES CHANGE IN SUPPORTING CHARACTERS

In many ways, the Elder is an obvious archetype. The idea of the old mentoring the young is familiar to us all. Yet the profundity of this archetype has somewhat faded from modern culture. Elders are no longer revered as they once were, and I daresay this is largely because few elders are truly Elders in the archetypal sense of someone who has completed all the initiations and arcs up to this point in the life cycle.

Wherever we encounter true Elder energy, we encounter something very special. We encounter the presence of a person who has the ability to not just guide or teach the younger generation, but to act as the very initiatory force that allows these younger characters to embark upon and complete their own journeys. (For example, it is no accident that it is often, and most famously, the subsequent impact archetype of the Mentor who "calls" the Hero to the quest.)

Many of our current Elder stories feature protagonists, such as Bill Murray's Vincent, who have *not* fully reached this stage archetypally and who therefore can offer only limited guidance and mentorship to their youngsters. Usually they are still trying to sort through their own unfinished business from their Second Act arcs. These stories certainly have their place, since they reflect reality and indeed may help society process its current struggles with initiatory arcs. However, a truly archetypal Elder story is one in which the Elder possesses not merely common-sense advice gleaned from life's experience, but more specifically a wisdom so deep it is in fact a latent power.

In *The Hero With a Thousand Faces*, Joseph Campbell recounts the beautiful Irish tale of four brothers who try to convince an old hag to give them water from her well. The three older brothers fail her tests because they fail to understand or respect the simple truth of her well-earned magnificence. Only the youngest brother, the pure-hearted Niall, succeeds and earns the right to be initiated by this true Elder when he willingly and cheerfully gives her the kiss she cannily requests.

Types of Story That Feature an Elder Protagonist

As with all of the Third-Act archetypes, it becomes more and more difficult to find well-executed examples that feature these characters as protagonists. We are much more likely to find them showing up as supporting Impact Characters in a younger protagonist's story.

These stories can span the gamut of possibilities, depending upon the type of change the younger character is undergoing. Most often, we find the Elder interacting with a Child (who as a fellow Flat archetype may also ingenuously offer certain truths to the Elder, which will aid the older character in the necessary healing and integration before the new trials of the Crone Arc), a Maiden, a Lover, a Parent, or a Queen.

The Elder isn't likely to interact with a Ruler or King, simply because the Elder is so recently and traumatically graduated from these archetypes. To get involved with figures of power would likely cause a regression. The Elder has just left the palace; the hut is where the Elder needs to be for this phase.

The Elder also isn't likely to interact with the Hero, since a Hero showing up at her door often signifies the Elder's own Call to Adventure within the Crone Arc. As we've seen, the Hero will very often accompany the Crone on her descent to the Underworld (such as in Pixar's *Up*).

As with most of the Flat archetypes, the Elder is likely to feature in a domestic story. Unlike the Change Arcs, which are at least symbolically about threats to the Kingdom (i.e., the "threat" of impending and necessary change), the Flat archetypes represent characters dealing with the mundane if no less dramatic trials of daily life.

Indeed, some of our Elders' most potent work is not even that of undergoing their own remaining transformation arcs, but simply offering back all they have earned and learned to guide the transitions of the younger arcs who follow in their footsteps.

Examples of the Elder

Examples of the Elder archetype include the following.

- John Jarndyce in *Bleak House*
- Ninny Threadgoode in *Fried Green Tomatoes*

- Aunt Trotwood in *David Copperfield*
- Vincent MacKenna in *St. Vincent*
- Harriett Lauler in *The Last Word*
- Sook in "A Christmas Memory"
- Queenie Turrill in *Larkrise to Candleford*

"Mentoring is an archetypal activity
that has timeless elements
which can connect us to the universal ground
where nature renews itself
and culture becomes reimagined.
Youth and elder meet where the pressure
of the future meets the presence of the past.
Old and young are opposites
that secretly identify with each other;
for neither fits well into the mainstream of life."
—Michael Meade

21

THE MENTOR

AND SO WE come to the final archetype within the life-arc cycle: the well-known and well-loved Mentor. This last Flat archetype, the one that precedes the final transformation of the Mage Arc, is deeply significant within human storytelling. Indeed, next to the Hero, the Mentor is perhaps our most well-known of all mythic archetypes.

The Wise Old Man shows up time and again: Obi-Wan, Gandalf, Dumbledore. Sans white beard, the Mentor need not be explicitly male, of course. The Mentor is simply a character who has advanced well into the elder phase and has won out in all the great tests of life. Unlike the previous Flat archetype of Elder, the Mentor is a character who has undertaken the first journey of life's Third Act—the Crone Arc—and risen above the physical limitations of old age into a transcendent wisdom and even power.

The Mentor character will have one more possible transformative Change Arc to undergo—that of the Mage's surrender of life itself. But for now this is a character who straddles the balance point of Life and Death and has come to a sober peace with both. As a result, the Mentor is in a prime position to not just *guide* the young, as did the previous archetype of Elder, but to *initiate* them by calling them into the quest.

The Mentor Archetype: Coming Full Circle

Previous Arc: Crone
Subsequent Arc: Mage
Subsequent Possible Negative Archetypes: Miser (passive); Sorcerer (aggressive)

As referenced in Chapter 16 about the first Flat archetype of the Child, the Mentor shares surprising commonalities with the young Innocent. The life cycle can be seen to represent a coming full circle—from Fool to Holy Fool. The Mentor, with all his or her hard-earned wisdom, represents if not a return to innocence, then at least a return to *understanding* it. What was lost in childhood has been regained but with the compounded interest of experience.

This makes the Mentor particularly fit to counsel the First-Act archetypes of Maiden and Hero, since by now the Mentor both knows what it was like to struggle with these life transitions and also that these youngsters must struggle *through* to transformation.

The challenge of the subsequent Mage Arc will be that of letting go of the world and the youngsters in his charge. But for the Mentor, that time has not yet come. This is why we see the Mentor prominently within the grand Kingdom-saving adventures of the Hero. Thanks to the just-completed Crone Arc, the Mentor has integrated the surrender of power in a healthy way that now allows a return to the heart of life's important power struggles. The Mentor is not King any longer; rather, the Mentor holds the more independent and in some ways even more powerful position of guiding the King, et al.

The Mentor is no longer confined to the palace as during the King Arc. Now the Mentor is free to wander the world, ever on a mission to protect what must soon be left behind. When the Mentor spies something amiss, he or she often becomes the messenger who arrives to tell King and Hero that trouble is on the way and must be dealt with.

The Mentor's Normal World

Symbolically, the Mentor's home is the entire Kingdom. This character wanders where he or she wills, seeming to neither have nor need any fixed residence. The Mentor is welcome wherever he or she goes, revered by all who are pure of heart and who can recognize the esteemed status of this worthy and wise elder.

Within most stories, the Mentor often offers at least a symbolic sense of magic. He or she often shows up out of nowhere, perhaps even a stranger to the younger characters, to help just as a threat to the Kingdom is rising.

Usually, the Mentor is distinct from the Elder in that the Elder lives in the hut on the edge of the woods, separate from but still a part of the village, still rooted to normal, mortal life. In contrast, the Mentor is a wanderer, coming and going as he or she pleases.

This is not always literally true within a story, especially modern stories. But because truly archetypal Mentors are so rare within our modern world, we almost always instinctively portray them as at least a little otherworldly. And so they do not tend to live within the confines of the Hero's Village or the King's Empire. They arrive, and they depart.

We can see this with Dumbledore in the Harry Potter series. Even though he lives in Hogwarts School, along with Harry and the other students, Headmaster Dumbledore is often away on his own business. He comes and goes as he pleases.

In other stories, such as *The Green Mile* and *Good Will Hunting*, the Mentor characters (John Coffey and Sean Maguire, respectively) live with or near the other characters for the duration of the story. But they are significant in that they arrive at the beginning of the story and then, in some way, depart at the end.

The Mentor's Relationship to the Thematic Truth

In completing the previous Crone Arc, the Mentor made the jump from wise Elder to a deeper and more transcendent understanding of Life and Death, a thematic Truth that might perhaps be phrased as: "Life is Death and Death is Life."

Most significantly, the completion of the Crone Arc has marked a coming to peace with impending death (however magically or prosaically you wish to frame that idea within your own story). This Truth is inherent not just within the Mentor's ability to guide younger archetypes through their own age-appropriate transformations, but also in symbolizing something greater and more profound to the up-and-coming world. Here at the end of life, the Mentor represents deeper meaning. The Mentor represents the promise to the younger archetypes that if they remain on course and do not give up, they too may follow the same path all the way to the end.

Chronologically, the Mentor is a very old character, near to the final arc and the end of the journey. Therefore, it is significant that the Mentor represents a character who has not given up on life or legacy. He or she has great purpose, perhaps more so than any of the preceding archetypes. In many ways, that purpose is defined by compassion for the younger archetypes.

In *The Hero With a Thousand Faces*, Joseph Campbell writes that the Mentor:

> ...does not abandon life. Turning his regard from the inner sphere of thought-transcending truth (which can be described only as "emptiness," since it surpasses speech) outward again to the phenomenal world, he perceives without the same ocean of being that he found within.... Having surpassed the delusions of his formerly self-assertive, self-defensive, self-concerned ego, he knows without and within the same repose.... And he is filled with compassion for the self-terrorized beings who live in fright of their own nightmare.

WRITING ARCHETYPAL CHARACTER ARCS | 263

How the Mentor Creates Change in Supporting Characters

The Mentor's role in impacting younger archetypes is perhaps the most obvious of all the Flat Archetypes: he or she *mentors* them. Specifically, we know from the familiar Hero's Journey that the Mentor is often the character who arrives at the would-be Hero's doorstep to call him to the adventure and initiate him on his journey.

It is worth noting, again, that even though all these archetypes can and do reference individual people, they are also significant as symbolic aspects of a single psyche (whether author, reader, protagonist—or all three). As such, the Mentor represents to the younger archetypes their own symbolic potential. Campbell notes that the Mentor is the Hero's "personification of his destiny to guide and aid him."

The Mentor is a character who demands change. The only reason a Mentor shows up in a story is to make something happen. Unlike other Flat archetypes (or even Change archetypes), who wait until the need for change demands they act, the Mentor is always a catalyst.

When the student is ready, the teacher appears.

That is the Mentor. And when the Mentor shows up, the student's life will be forever changed.

Types of Stories That Feature a Mentor Protagonist

The Mentor is, of course, prominent in stories that feature the Hero Arc. The Mentor can be seen to be most active in these stories, since he or she will often need to physically accompany the Hero at least part of the way.

On the other hand, if the Mentor is instead helping a King, the Mentor character is perhaps more likely to fill an advisory role, since the King is perfectly capable of taking action and fighting his own battles. Unlike the Hero, the King is more likely to recognize the Mentor's value and want to protect him or her from physical danger. (The Mentor may or may not need this protection, but will probably humor the King if only to give the King the opportunity to do his own transformative growth.)

Mentor stories are often big stories, since Mentors don't show up for any little old problem that can be handled by an earlier Flat archetype. This is perhaps why the Mentor is most prominent in Hero and King Arcs—since these two arcs mark the thresholds or "Doorways of No Return" (between the First and Second Act and the Second and Third Act, respectively).

Often, the "magical" quality of the Mentor lends itself to stories with a supernatural or fantastical bend. But even in stories with real-world settings, a Mentor character will often have psychic abilities or perhaps just a sixth sense.

Examples of the Mentor

Examples of the Mentor archetype include the following.

- John Coffey in *The Green Mile*
- Dr. Sean Maguire in *Good Will Hunting*
- Morpheus in *The Matrix*
- The White in The Lightbringer Series
- Glinda the Good Witch in *The Wizard of Oz*
- Obi-Wan Kenobi in *Star Wars: A New Hope*
- Albus Dumbledore in *Harry Potter and the Philosopher's Stone* (among others)
- Gandalf the White in *The Lord of the Rings*
- Mentor in *The Odyssey*
- Mrs. Whatsit, Mrs. Who, and Mrs. Which in *A Wrinkle in Time*
- Oogway in *Kung-Fu Panda*
- Soothsayer in *Kung-Fu Panda 2*
- Mr. Miyagi in *The Karate Kid*

Part 4: The Twelve Archetypal Antagonists

"ANTAGONIST, n.
The miserable scoundrel who won't let us."
—Ambrose Bierce

22

INTRODUCTION TO THE TWELVE ARCHETYPAL ANTAGONISTS

ANTAGONISTS ARE AN interesting consideration for any writer. So often when we conceive or plot a story, the antagonist may be an afterthought. This is especially so in genre or "plot-driven" fiction in which the antagonist is less likely to be in a relationship with the protagonist and more likely to be a "Big Bad" of some sort. And yet, in many ways, the antagonist in any type of story is the *point*. The antagonist is the reason there is a story at all. Without the antagonist—without opposition to the protagonist's forward progress or a catalyst to prompt the protagonist's growth—we don't have much of a story, do we?

The first three sections in this book discussed archetypes of Positive Change, Negative regression or stagnation, and resting or Flat archetypes. Many of these archetypes interact with each other as one another's antagonists. In particular, the negative shadow archetypes (such as the Tyrant and the Witch) can often be seen as both the inner and outer antagonists that positive archetypes (such as the Hero and the Queen) may have to overcome in order to complete their own character arcs.

Throughout, you may have also noticed references to certain archetypal antagonists that are more abstract and not always characterized as specific human antagonists in the same way as the "negative archetypes." In this final section, we will explore the twelve archetypal antagonists that can be found inherently within each of the six main archetypal life arcs. Following is an overview reminder of each of those arcs, as well as the adjoining archetypal antagonists we will be discussing in this section:

1. **The Maiden Arc** (Chapter 2)
   Archetypal Antagonists: Authority and Predator

2. **The Hero Arc** (Chapter 3)
   Archetypal Antagonists: Dragon and Sick King

3. **The Queen Arc** (Chapter 4)
   Archetypal Antagonists: Invader and Empty Throne

4. **The King Arc** (Chapter 5)
   Archetypal Antagonists: Cataclysm and Rebel

5. **The Crone Arc** (Chapter 6)
   Archetypal Antagonists: Death Blight and Tempter

6. **The Mage Arc** (Chapter 7)
   Archetypal Antagonists: Evil and the Weakness of Humankind

In future chapters, we will examine each antagonistic pairing more closely in relationship to the specific arcs. For now, I want to start with a quick overview of what these archetypal antagonists represent globally throughout the arcs.

What Is the Difference Between an Antagonist and an Antagonistic Force?

The overarching thematic antagonists within each arc or journey are clearly abstract forces: Dragon, Cataclysm, Death, Evil, etc. In certain types of stories, these abstract forces can be personified or anthropomorphized (e.g., Smaug the dragon in *The Hobbit* or Death in Harry Potter's "The Tale of the Three Brothers"). However, in more realistic stories, these forces can be symbolically represented by another human, a human system, or simply an abstraction that is never even named beyond the protagonist's inner struggle (e.g., the "Evil" faced by Will Smith's Mage character in *The Legend of Bagger Vance* is "merely" one man's loss of meaning and purpose after suffering in World War I).

This is where it becomes important to distinguish between an "antagonist" and an "antagonistic force." Defined simply, the antagonist in a story is whoever or whatever consistently creates obstacles between the protagonist and his or her ultimate plot goal. Although the archetypal antagonists we will be discussing in this section represent moral corruption of some sort, the word "antagonist" in itself never indicates any kind of moral alignment. It is possible for the antagonist to be the most moral person in the story and the protagonist the least moral (as is often the case in stories with Negative Change Arc protagonists).

The antagonist need not be human or even specifically conscious. However, the term "antagonist" can generally be used to distinguish a human (or humanized) antagonist, while the broader term "antagonistic force" can be used to indicate a more abstract form of obstacle to the protagonist's forward progression. More than that, it is both possible and prevalent to see a specific human antagonist "representing" a greater and more abstract antagonistic force. For example, in *The Lord of the Rings*, the Sorcerer Saruman is both a proxy for the greater antagonistic force of Sauron (a barely anthropomorphized representation of Evil) *and* a personal antagonist, acting on his own account, against whom the protagonists must do battle.

Antagonistic forces, even more than antagonists, have a tendency to be deeply thematic. They may even be nothing more or less within the story than a representation of the Lie the Protagonist Believes, which the protagonist must overcome in order to continue down a growthful path. Even if a protagonist must physically defeat a human antagonist in the end, that final outward battle is really only a representation (an externalized metaphor) of the defeat of the greater thematic antagonist. Therefore, it is often useful and even desirable to create a story that offers both an antagonistic force *and* a specific antagonist who can represent that abstract force within the actual plot conflict.

INNER AND OUTER ANTAGONISTS

The six main Positive Change life arcs offer up archetypal examples of *both* the thematic antagonistic force (e.g., the King's Cataclysm) and a more practical plot-based antagonist represented by another character or characters (e.g., the King's Rebels). Whether or not you choose to characterize these separately, they offer the opportunity to thoroughly examine your protagonist's inner and outer conflicts by uniting them in cohesion and resonance.

Which antagonist is represented in the outer conflict and which is primarily a concern of the inner conflict will depend on how you choose to dramatize your story's theme. For example, in a Maiden Arc, her inner conflict may concentrate on her own internalized sense of Authority while the Predator is externalized (as in *Jane Eyre*). Equally valid, however, would be the presentation of a disempowering and devouring Predator as her own inner critic, while she faces abusive or restrictive Authority in the external plot (as in *Little Dorrit*).

Really, they are two sides of the same coin—one representing the other but ultimately both representing the same thematic struggle. The emphasis of one over the other often depends on whether the story itself is more internal and relationship-driven or more external and action-driven. Regardless, your protagonist will confront both, in some guise, by the end. If the external antagonist is to be defeated in the Climax, it is usually because the protagonist has already conquered the internal antagonist. By the same token, if the inner conflict isn't much addressed within the story, then the destruction of the external antagonist can often be seen as a metaphor for the character's internal triumph over the greater antagonistic force.

Antagonists and Contagonists

In their Dramatica system of story theory, Chris Huntley and Melanie Anne Phillips coined the term "contagonist" to indicate an opposing force within the story who was not as *directly* opposed to the protagonist as the actual antagonist. Although sometimes the contagonist might be a direct, if undetected, proxy for the antagonist (akin to what John Truby calls a "false ally") the contagonist is just as likely to be a character who, at least on a plot level (if not a thematic one), is totally separate from the main antagonistic force.

The contagonist is a sort of "subplot antagonist," one who may be closer to the protagonist than the actual Big Bad antagonist and who therefore has more influence over the protagonist's internal conflict. The Dramatica system contrasts the contagonist with the "guardian" (i.e., a mentor-like character in a supporting-character role). Respectively, the two characters act as the competing "devil" and "angel" on the protagonist's shoulders, each seeking to be the Impact Character who influences the protagonist's thematic choices and determines whether the protagonist will remain in the Lie or evolve into the Truth.

The contagonist is contrasted with a mentor character because he, wittingly or unwittingly, seeks to ultimately hinder rather than help the protagonist. But the contagonist is different from the antagonist because he is not directly opposed to the protagonist's plot goal. The contagonist is someone who may be on the protagonist's side in the overall conflict, but who gets in the protagonist's way and causes the protagonist to consider backing out of the battle against the antagonist or taking the wrong moral path to the end goal.

Although the archetypal antagonist pairings we will be discussing will not always fall neatly into antagonist/contagonist roles, it is useful to keep this dynamic in mind as another way to examine the greater, more abstract thematic antagonistic *force* and the nearer, more intimate human antagonists who people your story.

Again, Saruman in *Lord of the Rings* presents a good example, in that he is a specific human antagonist who can be seen to fill that role across archetypes, depending on which characters are opposing him: Heroes, Queens, Crones, Mages, etc. For example, he can be seen variously as the Sick King whose realm is dying because of his neglect and whom the "Hero" Frodo must "heal," the Tyrant whom the "Queen" Aragorn must replace, and the Tempter whom the "Crone" Gandalf the Gray must resist.

Saruman is the proxy for the overarching antagonistic force represented by Sauron, but he is also operating on his own account, sometimes even in opposition to Sauron. His presence within the story allows the characters to confront different facets and embodiments of the overarching thematic antagonistic force, something that would not have been available had they merely faced the Big Bad Sauron.

In many ways, understanding your story's antagonist and/or antagonistic force is the key not just to understanding the plot but to understanding your story's true thematic significance, whether it is specifically following an archetypal plot or not.

"Authority is a solvent of humanity:
look at any husband, any father of a family,
and note the absorption of the person
by the persona, the individual by the role....
Surely man in general is born to be
oppressed or solitary, if he is to be fully human;
unless it so happens that he is
immune to the poison."
—Patrick O'Brian

23

Authority and Predator

AS WE EXPLORED in Chapter 2, the first transformational archetype within the life arcs cycle, the Maiden Arc, is the quintessential "coming-of-age" story. It is the story of teenage angst, the joys and heartbreaks of growing up, and the struggle to individuate into a fully autonomous and mature human being.

Like all arcs, the Maiden's doesn't just happen. Nor does she necessarily choose it—despite all her eagerness to turn sixteen and get her first car. Although humans can prepare themselves for transformational arcs, we don't get to initiate them for ourselves. The outer circumstances of our social environment and our own chronological progression through life are major factors in eventually creating the necessary forces to prompt a Change Arc. One way of viewing these circumstances is *as* the antagonistic force that defines both plot and theme in a life arc.

For the Maiden Arc, this antagonistic force can be seen archetypally as the Authority Figures who initiate her transition out of Childhood into the beginnings of the subsequent Hero Arc. Within her inner conflict (and sometimes externalized into the outer plot), we can see, too, that she also faces a frightening Predator—a fearsome doorkeeper that seems to prevent her from passing through the gates of adulthood.

The Maiden's Antagonists: Practical and Thematic

As mentioned in the previous chapter, there are actually multiple symbolic antagonists that can be seen as important within archetypal character arcs. Particularly, we can usually identify two—one that represents the protagonist's outer conflict and another that primarily symbolizes the inner conflict. Which is which will largely depend on the unique factors of your particular story.

Authority as an Archetypal Antagonist

Successfully initiating into adulthood is not merely a matter of passing through puberty or turning sixteen or twenty-one. On a deeper level, it is an initiation of the soul, a transition from the innocence and dependence of childhood into the complexity and responsibility of adulthood. Somewhat paradoxically, this initiation is driven by the Authority in the Maiden's life.

The paradox lies in the fact that this Authority *wants* the Maiden to undergo her arc and grow up. The Authority figures are inevitably those who encourage and even demand this transition. And yet the Authority figures are also those against whom the Maiden must struggle to escape.

It is always possible to represent these two facets of the Authority in different characters—representing the encouraging and initiatory Authority in a wise Parent or Elder, while representing the negative aspect of the selfish or smothering Authority in a shadow archetype such as the Sorceress or Tyrant. However, I think we can all recognize how both of these aspects usually reside within the same person. Loving parents will wish to see their children grow into responsible adults, even as there is a part of them that wants to maintain the Child in their care and control.

Therefore, it is important to recognize that although Authority is the archetypal antagonist within a Maiden Arc, that Authority isn't necessarily opposing her for evil or even purely selfish reasons.

In the Maiden Arc chapter, I mentioned that this Authority could potentially be characterized as either the Naïve Father or what Clarissa Pinkola Estés calls the "Too-Good Mother." What is meant by these titles is that the parents have come to represent, within the Maiden's maturation, a stagnation and/or completion of their ability to teach her. Even the best parents will eventually run the course of what they can pass on to their children; at a certain point the Maiden must always strike out to learn for herself.

This Authority can also be represented by other facets of society, such as teachers, religious leaders, or political figures. It can be represented abstractly by an "institution" or the "system." It can even be internalized into the Maiden's own evolving conscience. The loudest authoritarian voice, trying to convince her to remain in ignorance and irresponsibility, may be the voice inside her own head—telling her she doesn't know what she's doing, telling her she should just trust in those who know better, telling her she's better off doing what she's told. Indeed, this mindset can be the most formidable antagonist any Maiden faces. If not overcome, it can cause a person to remain unindividuated from Authority long into their lives.

The Predator as an Archetypal Antagonist

Authority is the more obvious archetypal antagonist that every Maiden must face. But there is another important opposing force in her arc: the Predator.

Classically, the Predator is best represented in such folk tales as "The Seven Wives of Bluebeard" and "The Girl Without Hands." Both of these stories feature a predatory masculine force that wishes to wed the Maiden. In the former, this Predator is the title character Bluebeard, who secretly murdered all his previous wives and kept their bodies locked in a hidden room. In the latter, it is the Devil, who chops off the Maiden's hands when she refuses him.

Symbolically, the Predator represents a seductive but toxic masculine presence. The Maiden, on the cusp of sexual awakening and a whole new world that she does not yet understand, starts out lacking the wisdom to discern between this toxic Predator and the worthy masculine as represented in the Protector.

Although often characterized by a love interest, the Predator's involvement with the Maiden need not be romantic or sexual. What he foundationally represents are the alluring dangers of the strange and exciting world "out there." In the beginning, the Maiden will not recognize that the Predator is essentially an extension of the dark side of that same Authority against whom she struggles to individuate. Should she fall prey to this controlling aspect of the masculine, marrying him will not gain her the independence she seeks. Instead, she will find herself entrenched deeper than ever within the very authoritarian structures beyond which she sought to evolve.

It is possible that wise Authority figures (from whom the Maiden nevertheless still needs to individuate) may recognize the Predator's threat and offer counsel (which will go at least partially unheeded) against the Maiden's involvement with him. However, as in the mentioned folk tales, it is customary that the Authority figures collude with the Predator's plan to take the Maiden as wife. This could arise from a selfish desire to bind the Maiden further into their control or to their advantage (such as with Rose's mother in *Titanic*, a woman who explicitly opposes her daughter's individuation by demanding she marry a rich but brutal man), or it could be that the "Naïve Father" and "Too-Good Mother" (such as seen in the story of "The Girl Without Hands" and so many other fairy tales about cursed babies) are simply too foolish or enslaved themselves to recognize or oppose the Predator's proposal to their daughter.

It is also important to recognize that the Predator is ultimately representative of a psychological aspect within the Maiden herself as she undertakes this journey. The Predator is the inner critic, the voice inside her young head telling her she is not good enough, smart enough, or brave enough to see through the devil's tricks and make it through the wilderness on her own. Indeed, in many stories, the Predator may be *most* representative of the protagonist's inner struggle against her own insecurities and fears. Growing up, after all, is scary business, and often the dark and dominating parts of ourselves are our most formidable antagonists.

How the Maiden's Archetypal Antagonists Operate in the Conflict and the Climactic Moment

The antagonist's most basic role is to generate the plot conflict. The antagonist does this by consistently creating opposition/obstacles to the protagonist's progress toward the plot goal. Via these obstacles, the protagonist is forced to reconsider her mode of being, her belief structures, and her tactics. The antagonist's opposition forces her to evolve—thus allowing for an externalized story that also creates personal transformation within the protagonist.

In the Maiden Arc, the protagonist's plot goal may be any number of things (graduating from high school, getting a job, running away from home, staying at home, attracting a love interest's attention, learning a new skill, surviving a disaster, etc.). But the thematic goal will always be that of growing up, of gaining a certain measure of independence, autonomy, and personal responsibility.

This means the archetypal antagonists within a Maiden Arc are always fundamentally opposed, in some way, to her growing up. It is possible they are aligned ultimately with her maturation (what parents don't want their child to graduate from high school, after all?), but just not the *way* in which the Maiden is going about it (e.g., maybe she wants to go to a different college than the parent's alma mater).

What is important is that the protagonist will want something that represents or enables her eventual individuation and initiation into adulthood—and the Authority antagonist will create obstacles, even if they are well-intentioned (such as Jess's traditional parents in *Bend It Like Beckham*, who just want her to be happy and successful in the usual ways for their culture).

The Predator's presence may be more complicated. Usually, he will act more as a contagonist—a seemingly wiser Impact Character who appears to offer the protagonist what she's looking for (in this case, a way out of her childhood into a new mode of being). But a true Predator will eventually prove himself also an obstacle to the protagonist's individuation. She may realize that in order to individuate from the Authority, she will have to individuate from the Predator as well. (Although, as with Mr. Rochester in *Jane Eyre*, it is always possible the Predator may be redeemed after he recognizes his controlling ways and instead blesses the protagonist's growth.)

Which of your archetypal antagonistic forces is the true antagonist in your story will depend on which is finally overcome in the Climactic Moment. Usually, the "subplot" antagonist will be overcome previously, but it is also possible that the true showdown in the Climactic Moment will allow for an easy resolution of the secondary conflict afterwards.

Unless the Authority in your story is truly malignant (as represented by older shadow archetypes), it is likely that the Maiden's transformation will "renew the Kingdom." Parents and other Authority Figures will themselves grow through the Maiden's initiation. They will recognize her as a burgeoning adult and an equal, they will step out of her way, and they will probably bless her future life by wishing her only the best.

In many ways, the Maiden Arc is the most relational of all the life arcs, since its archetypal antagonist is one that in most humans' lives is not corrupted, just restrictive. Authority only becomes the "bad guy" when it is selfishly opposed to necessary growth. Perhaps more than any of the other intrinsic antagonistic forces, the Maiden's antagonists offer the opportunity for the strongest growth arcs of their own, since the Maiden's transformation may inspire them to take their own arcs. Indeed, the transformational arc that follows the static archetype of Parent is that of Queen, which is all about growing into a true leadership that allows for and encourages the independence and responsibility of those in one's charge.

Examples of the Authority and Predator Archetypes

Examples of the Authority and Predator archetypes include the following.

Authority

- Rodmilla De Ghent in *Ever After*
- Mae Caldwell in *Secondhand Lions*
- Mrs. Henry Vale in *Now, Voyager*
- Mr. and Mrs. Bhamra in *Bend It Like Beckham*
- Edward Dorrit in *Little Dorrit*
- Ruth Dewitt Bukater in *Titanic*
- Mr. and Mrs. Foster in *Tuck Everlasting*
- Malik Khan in *Blinded by the Light*

Predator

- Pierre Le Pieu in *Ever After*
- The Terminator in *The Terminator*
- Edward Rochester in *Jane Eyre*
- Yubaba in *Spirited Away*
- Cal Hockley in *Titanic*
- The Man in the Yellow Suit in *Tuck Everlasting*
- Jareth in *Labyrinth*

"...there is a desolated country, a wasteland,
where cattle do not reproduce,
crops won't grow, knights are killed,
children are orphaned, maidens weep,
and there is mourning everywhere.
[T]he country's problems are related
to the wounded Fisher King,
who suffers continuously
because his wound will not heal."
—Jean Shinoda Bolen, M.D.

24

DRAGON AND SICK KING

THE WELL-KNOWN Hero Arc offers us the exciting story of a brave youth fighting to discover and earn his own worthiness. It follows on the heels of the Maiden Arc's initial individuation from the Authority that dominates one's youth. Now, the young adult receives the opportunity to discover what he is meant to do with his life.

Viewed mythically, the Hero Arc is usually an epic quest, in which the Hero ventures away from the Kingdom to confront a Dragon and find the elixir that will heal the Sick King and save the Kingdom. More realistically, it is a story about finding meaning and setting one's course in the very specific ways that will influence the entire rest of one's life.

As discussed in Chapter 3, the Hero Arc is a story about exploring one's newly burgeoning power as an adult—and discovering whether or not that power will be surrendered into a greater love. This love could be for a specific person or cause, but generally represents a loving reintegration with society itself.

As such, the Hero Arc is certainly a story with a deep inner conflict and character arc for the protagonist. The antagonists the character faces in the external plot may demand all sorts of heroic action. But fundamentally, as always, they represent key aspects of the Hero himself. The two faces of the Hero's archetypal antagonist are the Dragon and the Sick King. As always, one or the other can be more prevalent in the outer conflict, depending on the nature and focus of the specific tale. Either way, both are important symbolic forces within this exciting story.

The Hero's Antagonists: Practical and Thematic

Although the distinction may not always be cut and dried, we can recognize that a "practical" antagonist is one that faces the Hero in the external plot while a "thematic" antagonist is one that represents the character's inner struggle. Often, there is much crossover within the actual portrayal since of course we want plot and theme to be as unified as possible. When viewed symbolically through the terms Dragon and Sick King, we get a better glimpse of the true essence and purpose of these driving forces in a Hero's story.

Dragon as an Archetypal Antagonist

The symbolism of the Hero slaying the Dragon is one of the oldest in human memory. We recognize this representation of the Dragon as that of a "monster"—a relatively undifferentiated evil but one that is animalistic rather than abstract. In light of the fact that this "evil" will become *increasingly* abstract as the life arcs progress, it is interesting to consider that the Dragon appears as such a practical foe in the Hero Arc in part because youthful protagonists tend to view good and evil in very simple and practical terms—as another living entity that simply needs to be vanquished.

Other than being powerful, ravenous, and indiscriminately murderous, Dragons are generally portrayed as greedy hoarders. By the time the Call to Adventure reaches the unlikely Hero, it is clear the Dragon's threat to the Kingdom is less about whatever damage he is wreaking through his fire-breathing and more specifically about the problems resulting from something crucial he has stolen and/or hoarded.

WRITING ARCHETYPAL CHARACTER ARCS | 293

This special MacGuffin—famously referred to by Joseph Campbell as the "elixir"—could be a magical object, or it could be a person such as the princess whom the Hero is so often charged with saving. Whatever it is, it is more than just a "thing." It is symbolic of the Kingdom's well-being. Without this thing or person, the Kingdom will suffer and decay.

And so the Dragon represents a force in the Hero's world that is blocking health and growth. Crucially, the Dragon is blocking not just the Hero but others as well. The Hero Arc is founded upon the Hero learning to care for and protect others—in essence to become a stand-up member of society. As such, it is important that even in a relatively mundane story, the threat will be to *more* than just himself, even if it should seem that narrow in the beginning. Indeed, by the end, the Hero must become willing to sacrifice his own well-being for the good of all.

Depending on the scope of your story, the Dragon may indeed be an actual dragon or some other mythic foe. His essence can also be represented in other character archetypes, ranging from a Sorcerer on down to those shadow archetypes who are more properly the Hero's "equal" such as the Bully.

What is important is that the Dragon represents a threat to the Hero's safe little village world. It is a threat that initially seems far beyond the young Hero's capability to deal with. It is in the rising up that he reaches his heroic potential and grows into the caring responsibility and leadership of a mature adult.

The Sick King as an Archetypal Antagonist

Almost as ancient although perhaps less well-known than the Dragon is the Sick King. Very often in the old tales, the Hero Arc is precipitated by the illness of the realm's King. The magical object held by the Dragon is symbolically the healing elixir needed to cure the King.

It is understood the Sick King is representative of a sick Kingdom—that, indeed, the Kingdom's current woes are *because* of the King's sickness. Although this sickness may be a literal physical malady, it too is symbolic—of a failure of leadership or even egregious corruption on the King's part. He is no longer a true and healthy King, as we see in the King Arc, but more properly Puppet/Tyrant, or even Hermit/Witch or Miser/Sorcerer.

The Sick King represents a failure in the cycle of the life arcs. Because growth has stagnated, it falls upon the youthful life-force energy of a newly appointed Hero to try to right the balance (with perhaps some help from a canny Elder or Mentor). In the grotesque face of this corruption of responsible and loving leadership, the only hope is that either a rising Queen shall dethrone the Sick King, or a Hero shall redeem him. It is the Hero's purity and potential that allow him the opportunity to restore youth and vitality to the King and the Kingdom.

Although not healed as part of a Hero Arc, an excellent example of the Sick King can be found in *The Two Towers*, in which Theoden, king of Rohan, has lost all strength, vitality, and even reason due to the corrupting whispers of Wormtongue in his ear. The Kingdom suffers direly, on the brink of falling to the great Evil of Sauron, even as Theodon's son and heir dies and his beloved niece and nephew are degraded before him.

In some stories, the Sick King may only be a background motivation for the Hero's quest against the Dragon. The archetype of the Sick King may be mostly present within the story simply as evidenced in the sickness of the Kingdom through which the Hero travels. But the Sick King may also be a more direct antagonist.

If the Sick King's "illness" is less debilitating than corrupting, he may be represented as a powerful figure who is harming the Kingdom either personally or vicariously, through a weaponized Dragon (symbolic or otherwise). We can see this in all of the Baratheon and Lannister rulers in the *Game of Thrones* series, as well as in Daenerys Targaryen, who by the series' end is destroying the kingdom with a *literal* dragon.

It's also possible, and more mythically accurate, that the Sick

WRITING ARCHETYPAL CHARACTER ARCS | 295

King and the Dragon should both be actively destructive elements within the story, but ones who also directly oppose *each other*. In this case, the Hero may need to defeat them both in order to redeem the Kingdom.

How the Dragon and the Sick King Operate in the Conflict and the Climactic Moment

Like all the masculine arcs, the Hero Arc lends itself most obviously to plot-driven stories in which the primary antagonists are those faced in the external conflict. Indeed, it is possible the conflict should be entirely focused on external antagonists (which can still be deeply symbolic in their own right), but because this is specifically a Hero *Arc*, the changes should be influencing the protagonist's personal growth as well.

Both the Dragon and the Sick King will be active in the external plot. Often, the Sick King will be a presence lurking behind the Hero, pursuing him on his quest, while the Dragon lies in wait ahead of the Hero, creating obstacles. This can present a wonderfully layered set of conflicts, as well as many opportunities for raising the stakes.

Additionally, *both* the Dragon and the Sick King will be internal forces with which the Hero starts out unwittingly identifying. For example, just as Luke Skywalker in *The Empire Strikes Back* cuts down his vision of Darth Vader only to find his own face staring out of the broken mask, the Sick King represents the personal decay of the heroic principle.

Because the Hero's central struggle is between power and love—control and surrender—his relationship to the Sick King can be used to represent his own natural affinity and temptation toward corrupted Power. This struggle, of course, can end with a powerful declaration such as Luke's to Emperor Palpatine in *Return of the Jedi* when he later refuses to kill Vader, whom he now knows to be his own father: "I'll never turn to the Dark Side. You've failed, Your Highness. I am a Jedi, like my father before me."

The same holds true in regard to the Dragon. Symbolically, it is understood that the ancient Dragon was often simply another guise of the princess whom the Hero was trying to recognize and rescue. As such, the Dragon is in fact representative of the corrupted capacity for love within the Hero himself. His journey is that of overcoming his own selfishness and desire for power and control so he may love fully and compassionately. Only once he has slain his own inner Dragon is he worthy to love and save the princess and thereby heal the Kingdom. In their book *Romancing the Shadow*, Connie Zweig and Steve Wolf note:

> In these countless tales, a young male full of bravado makes a perilous journey, which typically includes a descent to darkness, slays a terrible shadow-monster, winning a damsel as his prize. Interpreted psychologically, the hero slays the monster-Other within; the ego vanquishes the shadow but does not stop to recognize it as a dark brother, so the deeper initiation does not take place.

These deeper initiations will wait until later arcs.

In most Hero Arc stories, the Dragon will be the final climactic antagonist the Hero faces. From there, he will return with the elixir to heal the Sick King in the Resolution. These trappings are, of course, deeply symbolic and can be maneuvered into many different practical aspects in different types of stories.

Foundationally, the Hero Arc is a wonderfully simple story about the struggle between love and power. As such, the conflict between protagonist and antagonist is usually relatively simple as well. There's a deep resonance and beauty to this, but it's important to recognize and remember that this simplistic view of good and evil (and life itself) is still a relatively youthful perspective. It is one that belongs specifically to the Hero stage of life and that should hopefully be moved past as the character continues to evolve into the capacity to see life's conflict in broader terms and to adapt accordingly to the archetypal antagonists yet to come.

WRITING ARCHETYPAL CHARACTER ARCS | 297

EXAMPLES OF THE DRAGON AND SICK KING ARCHETYPES

Examples of the Dragon and Sick King archetypes include the following.

Dragon

- Wicked Witch of the West in *The Wizard of Oz*
- Green Goblin alter-ego in *Spider-Man* (2002)
- Loki Odinson in *Thor*
- Biff Tannen in *Back to the Future*
- Gentleman With the Thistledown Hair in *Jonathan Strange and Mr. Norrell*
- The Death Star in *Star Wars*

Sick King

- Theoden in *The Two Towers*
- Darth Vader in *Star Wars*
- Wizard in *The Wizard of Oz*
- Norman Osborn in *Spider-Man* (2002)
- Long John Silver in *Treasure Island*
- President Snow in *The Hunger Games*
- Odin Borson in *Thor*
- George McFly in *Back to the Future*
- Gilbert Norrell in *Jonathan Strange and Mr. Norrell*
- Tom Dunson in *Red River*

"Remember that all through history,
there have been tyrants and murderers,
and for a time, they seem invincible.
But in the end, they always fall.
Always."
—Mahatma Gandhi

25

INVADER AND EMPTY THRONE

AS THE THIRD of the life cycle's archetypal character arcs, the Queen Arc is that of the mature adult who has completed the youthful arcs of Maiden and Hero and is now challenged to grow into a position of greater responsibility and leadership. This is the tale of someone who has so far proven herself worthy of love and responsibility in relationship, community, and perhaps parenthood. Now life calls for a further transformation—into capably accepting a true position of power.

The Queen Arc (see Chapter 4) is the sequel to the well-known Hero Arc both mythically in the sense that "what happens after" the Hero Arc is often the victorious Hero being given a position of leadership. More prosaically, it can be seen simply in the life of a modern person who has successfully "grown up" (with the Hero's quest signified by perhaps going to college, getting married, or committing to a career) and who is now beginning to tend the needs of the up-and-coming generation.

If the Hero Arc was about reconciling the potential for power with the goodness of love, the Queen Arc then is about recognizing that leadership requires not just love but also the ability to create order. As such, the Queen's archetypal antagonists are represented by the twofold threat of Invaders from beyond her happy home and the Empty Throne that fails to protect her and her family. Together, these two antagonistic forces catalyze the need for this next transformative arc. There is a dearth of leadership in the Kingdom, and she is being called to fulfill it.

The Queen's Antagonists: Practical and Thematic

Once again, we can see in these dualistic archetypal antagonists the two faces of a story's conflict: outer and inner, plot and theme. One represents the main thrust of the external conflict—whatever or whoever is framing the larger conflict and therefore the need for the Queen's ultimate plot goal of protecting or furthering those who depend upon her. The other antagonistic force represents more specifically the protagonist's inner drama—the inner obstacles that are both driving and blocking her ability to become the person she needs to be in order to triumph in the external conflict.

Usually in a Queen Arc, the Invader represents the outer antagonist, and the Empty Throne represents the inner antagonist. However, as with all of these symbolic antagonists, it is possible to achieve many flexible dynamics. For example, if the Empty Throne is truly empty, it may be an antagonistic force represented almost entirely by the Queen's own insecurities or inner resistance to sitting upon that throne. But if the throne is empty symbolically, in the sense that the current leadership is corrupt, then she may face a Tyrant character (perhaps in a contagonist role) who must be defeated before she can truly save the Kingdom from the Invaders.

Invader as Archetypal Antagonist

The Queen Arc is just one step up from the very dualistic mindset of the Hero Arc, in which the Hero faced the "evil other" of the animalistic Dragon. The Queen's primary external antagonist is also fundamentally viewed as "other," although this time the antagonist is at least humanized. Be-

WRITING ARCHETYPAL CHARACTER ARCS | 303

cause the Queen's purview of life is still comparatively small (i.e., the Kingdom), she starts out still operating from an "us vs. them" mindset. Her heart belongs to her people and only her people. And so when a threat arrives from outside the Kingdom, it is accepted as a danger to all she holds dear. In all likelihood, this antagonistic force of Invader will also be operating from this same "us vs. them" mindset, although more aggressively than defensively.

As such, there is certainly room within the Queen Arc to explore broadening mindsets. The Queen may end her story by subduing the Invaders, but she may also come to terms with them (now that she has transitioned into a fully realized Ruler) by inviting them into the protection of her Kingdom as equals rather than conquests. Regardless, part of the Queen's transformation is that of mentally moving into a larger setting. She begins her story feeling safe within the walls of the Kingdom and ends by looking beyond the walls to the larger realm to which she is now accountable and responsible.

What is most foundational to the Invader as an archetypal antagonist is that it begins the story by presenting a real threat to the home life the Queen has built and which she holds so dear. She probably has no real desire to become a Ruler (or, if she does, she struggles with its ambitious shadow aspects). It is the Invader who catalyzes the necessity of her growth. If she wishes to protect what she has built, she must now expand her capabilities.

Empty Throne as Archetypal Antagonist

If the throne were not empty, there would be no need for the Queen to undergo her arc. The responsibility of defending the Kingdom from Invaders doesn't yet fall upon her shoulders, but when she faithfully looks to the existing leadership paradigm to protect her and her people, she discovers the throne is empty.

This may not be an instantaneous discovery. Gradually, it will become clear to both the Queen and her children that nobody is helming the ship. Or if someone *is* steering, he is doing either a wretchedly incompetent or a criminally corrupt job of it.

The Invader represents the catalyst that prompts the Queen's journey, but it is the Empty Throne that demands she complete it. However happy she may (or may not) be to act as the Ruler's lieutenant, there is in fact no true Ruler for her to support. If she's going to achieve her plot goal and defend the needs of her family, she will have to rise to the task herself.

Often, the Empty Throne will be represented by a Tyrant character who must be overthrown in order to protect the Kingdom from the larger threat of the Invader. Although the Tyrant may indeed damage the Kingdom in his own right, he is not initially so great a threat that he immediately prompts the Queen to confront him. He is perhaps more a petty tyrant than a violent one (if the latter, then he could likely be considered an Invader in his own right). Most importantly, the Tyrant proves himself the obstacle standing between the Queen and the defeat of the Invaders.

It's also important to note that the Empty Throne need not always be representative of an evil force (i.e., of negligence or corruption). Because the Queen Arc marks a healthy and necessary progression in life, there is implicit within the arc the understanding that the throne *must* be cyclically vacated. Indeed, as we explored in Chapter 5, the King Arc is that of willingly stepping down from power for the good of all.

The Queen may be preceded by a good King, one who has faithfully sacrificed his leadership to protect his Kingdom. Indeed, he may do so in congruence with the Queen's own arc. In this case, the Empty Throne will be a naturally arising challenge for the Queen to grow into. Even in this scenario, the Empty Throne remains representative of an antagonistic force because it signifies the Queen's inner resistance to fully accepting this throne. When offered the crown, she may, like Prince Henry in *Ever After*, declare, "I don't want it!" Or she may be wary of her own tyrannical proclivities should she be given so much power over other people's lives—such as with Aragorn, in the film versions of *The Lord of the Rings*, who fears his lineage's weakness for the Ring's dark power.

How the Invader and the Empty Throne Operate in the Conflict and the Climactic Moment

The Invader will usually be the primary actor in the external conflict, even if it is just a framing conflict. Although the bulk of a story's scenes may be about the dynamic between the Queen and the Empty Throne, the central thrust of the plot is still toward and in response to the Invader. The "invasion" may be featured in many different guises, everything from the slow advance of a literal enemy force to the encroaching deadline for a neighborhood's destruction to a high school presidential campaign against a brazen newcomer. Whatever the case, this is the primary obstacle the Queen is focused on, in ways large and small, on every page of the story.

Although the Empty Throne may be one of many obstacles she faces on her route to fending off the Invader, it will be the *main* obstacle. As such, it may well feature in the majority of the book's scenes as the Queen grapples with either overthrowing a Tyrant and/or claiming her own true leadership capacity in order to do what is necessary to defend the Kingdom.

The Invader will likely be the primary antagonist defeated in the Climactic Moment. Even if the Queen has yet to officially take the throne upon defeating the Invaders, her defeat of the Empty Throne will not be the Climactic Moment. The only exception is if the Tyrant and the Invader are represented by the same character, in which case she will, of course, defeat both archetypes simultaneously.

Although the classic symbolism of this story indicates the Queen will repel the Invader by force and literally take the throne, becoming an uncontested leader, the actual stories need not be so simplistic. Instead of subjugating the Invaders, she may reconcile with them, either inviting them under her protection as subjects of her realm or respecting them as a sovereign nation in their own right. It may also be that she does not take someone else's physical throne, but simply learns to inhabit the Empty Throne in her own heart, embodying true sovereignty without necessarily ruling over a specific kingdom or people (family, business, etc.).

In whatever way the archetypal antagonists of Invader and Empty Throne manifest in your Queen Arc story, what is most important is that they represent the catalytic necessity for the Queen's own growth into a true servant-leader.

Examples of the Invader and Empty Throne Archetypes

Examples of the Invader and Empty Throne archetypes include the following.

Invader

- Mary of Guise in *Elizabeth*
- Old Man Potter in *It's a Wonderful Life*
- The English in *Joan of Arc*
- Voldemort in *Harry Potter and the Order of the Phoenix*
- Sauron in *The Return of the King*
- League leadership in *A League of Their Own*
- Syndrome in *The Incredibles*

Empty Throne

- Queen Mary and the Duke of Norfolk (among others) in *Elizabeth*
- Uncle Billy in *It's a Wonderful Life*
- King Charles VII in *Joan of Arc*
- Professor Umbridge in *Harry Potter and the Order of the Phoenix*
- Denethor in *The Return of the King*
- Commodus in *Gladiator*
- Jimmy Dugan in *A League of Their Own*
- Rick Dicker in *The Incredibles*

"And she thought then how strange it was
that disaster—the sort of disaster
that drained the blood from your body
and took the air out of your lungs
and hit you again and again in the face—
could be at times, such a thing of beauty."
—Anita Shreve

26

CATACLYSM AND REBEL

THE KING ARC begins the second half of the life cycle of archetypal character arcs. This placement as the fourth of six arcs necessarily makes it a turning point within the overarching "story structure" of life. We can recognize this particularly in the King's relationship to his archetypal antagonists.

The first three arcs—those of Maiden, Hero, and Queen—are primarily concerned with gaining power. The final three arcs—those of King, Crone, and Mage—are primarily concerned with surrendering power. As such, the early arcs often demonstrate comparatively narrow and dualistic views of the antagonistic forces that oppose them. For the young Maiden, the entire thrust of her transformation is that of individuating from Authority and becoming a separate person. The Hero then faces a dehumanized antagonistic force represented by the Dragon. And the Queen, although beginning to recognize her antagonist of Invader as her equal, still pushes back with an "us vs. them" mindset.

By the time we reach the challenges of the King Arc (see Chapter 5), this relationship to the antagonist begins to dramatically shift. The central challenge of the King Arc is that of recognizing a larger realm of power and potential, beyond the physical sphere on which he has so far spent all his focus.

As the successful Ruler of a vast Kingdom, he has necessarily moved beyond the Queen's small "us vs. them" mindset to recognize the interconnectedness of himself and all the subjects within his realm.

In *King, Warrior, Magician, Lover*, Robert Moore and Douglas Gillette note:

> The good king always mirrored and affirmed others who deserved it. He did this by seeing them—in a literal sense, in his audiences at the palace, and in the psychological sense of noticing them, knowing them, in their true worth. The good king delighted in noticing and promoting good men to positions of responsibility within his kingdom. He held audience, primarily, not to be seen (although this was important to the extent that he carried people's own projected inner King energy), but to see, admire, and delight in his subjects, to reward them and to bestow honors upon them.

Therefore, it is interesting to observe that the King's archetypal antagonists are much more connected to him than any that have come before, and that indeed much of his arc is about recognizing and even consecrating this connection.

The King faces the archetypal antagonists of Cataclysm and Rebel, both of which present challenges that ask him to culminate his rule in a way that blesses his Kingdom—even as he himself must journey on into the misty and liminal spaces of the Third Act of elderhood.

THE KING'S ANTAGONISTS: PRACTICAL AND THEMATIC

As ever, the concept of archetypal antagonists is rooted in deeply symbolic language. In an equally symbolic story, such as those in the fantasy genre, these antagonists may be realized literally. But in more realistic stories, such as those set in our modern world, these antagonistic forces can be recognized as just that—forces.

The Cataclysm, particularly, is a force. It represents a supernatural power descending upon the Kingdom and demanding

WRITING ARCHETYPAL CHARACTER ARCS | 313

the King evolve his tactics. Up to this point, the King has successfully defended his Kingdom from any number of "natural" enemies. In essence, he began his career back when he was the Queen staving off the threat of Invaders from without. Up to now, his "strong right arm" and the "sword of his mind" have proven more than capable of dealing with all comers.

Now the advent of the Cataclysm signals he is being called into his next arc. Much like the Invaders in the previous Queen Arc, the Cataclysm represents a threat from "beyond" and therefore one that creates the external conflict within the plot. Meanwhile, it is the King's own subjects who represent the threat from within the Kingdom. Some of them will become Rebels—disgruntled by the changing times, still lacking in maturity, and frightened of this Cataclysm which they are as yet unequipped to comprehend.

Cataclysm as Archetypal Antagonist

As with all the primary and external antagonists within these arcs, the Cataclysm is the reason the protagonist is being challenged to undertake this stage in his evolution. If this challenge were never to arrive and alter the status quo, there would be no reason (and arguably no ability) for the character to change.

The Cataclysm represents a particularly powerful antagonistic force. Partly, this is due to its awesomely destructive nature. As the first of the "spiritual" antagonists (followed by the Death Blight in the Crone Arc and Evil in the Mage Arc), the Cataclysm inevitably feels a bit apocalyptic. Mostly, this is due to its unprecedented and therefore unknown nature. This is like nothing the protagonist has faced before; or, more practically, it is something against which all the old successful methods will not work.

More personally to the King, the Cataclysm simply represents the turning of the tide within his own life. He is growing older. He is approaching the end of his physical vigor. Even though old age and death may yet be decades in the future, he is now closer to his death than to his birth.

And so, although the Cataclysm may indeed be represented

as a supernatural force, it may also be represented in a quieter or more realistic story as simply the character's need to grapple with the end of an era within his job or family life.

In the beginning of the story, the King will see the Cataclysm as an enemy, perhaps even accepting a narrative in which this force is malignant and deliberately out to get him or his subjects. Because his story is one in which he is being asked to leave his throne (willingly or not), he will have to acknowledge and deal with feelings of resistance and resentment.

If he succeeds in facing this antagonist, he will come to realize its antagonism is not personal. Indeed, the Cataclysm is a supernatural force. Even though its consequences are frightening, it is in fact a messenger warning the King of changes that must be made if the balance of his own and his subjects' health is to be maintained.

Symbolically, the only way to defeat the Cataclysm and protect the Kingdom from its threatened apocalypse is for the King to sacrifice himself to restore balance. The Cataclysm is not out to get him; rather, it is offering him the opportunity to avoid destruction. As such, the King will come to realize the Cataclysm is less an enemy than a strange friend.

Rebel as Archetypal Antagonist

Why must the King give up his throne? A true King is a good King. Seems like we should keep him on his throne as long as possible, right?

First of all, keep in mind that just because someone reaches the positive archetypal stage of Ruler does not mean he will ever be called to take the transformational King Arc. Some people will spend their elder years in the Flat archetype of Ruler (see Chapter 19), never taking the final three arcs. This isn't necessarily a bad thing, since whether or not someone is called to fulfill these archetypes can depend largely on contextual social needs. No one's archetypal journeys take place within a vacuum.

If the King is indeed called upon this transformative journey, in which the Cataclysm signals an impending and destructive imbalance within the Kingdom, it is likely because it is time for

WRITING ARCHETYPAL CHARACTER ARCS | 315

his young subjects to rise into their own roles of leadership. If the King were to refuse to step aside to make way for the new Queens and, by extension, if he were to refuse to take his own initiations into elderhood and therefore remain incapable of further initiating the younger Maidens and Heroes—he would block the growth of the overall Kingdom. Stagnation and rot would set in: Cataclysm.

We can see the results of this failure on the King's part in that he often shows up in the negative shadow aspect of Tyrant in Queen stories. But we also see his inner conflict with this reality even within his own successful arc.

In any King Arc, younger characters will be prominent and important. If the King's story is about leaving the throne, then there must be someone to whom he passes the crown—worthy Heroes and Queens who will benefit from his stalwart legacy. But there will also be Rebels. These characters represent an antagonistic force *within* the Kingdom. Catalyzed by the fearsome Cataclysm—which they, unlike the true King, lack the wisdom to understand—they distrust the King's responses to this emergency. The Rebels ultimately represent that part of the King's psyche that also wants to rebel against this new reality and that seeks power by any means.

Externalized, the Rebels deepen the complexity of the narrative by providing a convincing argument for the King *not* to abandon his throne and sacrifice himself to the Cataclysm. After all, these rowdy upstarts are clearly unready to replace him in all his wisdom and experience.

Depending on the nature of the story, the Rebels may be redeemed into worthy successors—or they may be defeated by those among the King's subjects who *are* worthy to take up his crown.

How the Cataclysm and Rebels Operate in the Conflict and the Climactic Moment

Usually, the Cataclysm will represent the outer conflict—the main problem the protagonist is trying to solve. This could be a literal apocalypse or it could be the dissolution of the character's business, or it could be an illness such as cancer or Alzheimer's that is threatening the character's previous mode of life.

Almost always, the Cataclysm will be presented as something abstract. The enemy will not be human even if it employs a human army. Alternatively, the "mastermind" might be a mortal who unwittingly wields a supernatural power he does not fully understand and which escapes the leash. The Cataclysm is a deep existential problem, but it is not a person or group of people who can be easily vilified.

By contrast, the Rebels are almost always human characters close to the King. While the Cataclysm represents the antagonist, the Rebels are more likely to represent the contagonist—a force that is not directly opposed to the King but which starts out seemingly aligned with him only to try to tempt him off his true path.

The Rebels offer much opportunity for thematic complexity and depth, since they can be represented by both shadow archetypes as well as positive-but-simply-immature archetypes. In short, although the Rebels may indeed be aggressive shadow archetypes—Bullies and Sorceresses—who wish to usurp the power of the throne for their own means, they may also simply be well-meaning young upstarts who don't yet "know that they don't know."

Ultimately, all varieties of Rebels are the King's subjects, and he will feel an alignment with them and a call to protect and serve them. It is very possible for even far-gone Rebels to be redeemed by the King's sacrifice in the end, such as seen with the character of Edmund Pevensie in C.S. Lewis's allegory *The Lion, the Witch, and the Wardrobe*.

The Climactic Moment in a King story will be his sacrifice—that moment when he surrenders himself to the warning of the Cataclysm and gives his life to right the balance of his Kingdom. Depending on how the Rebels are represented within the story, this sacrifice on the King's part may instantly redeem them—or defeat them. It's also possible the Rebels will be dealt with in the Climax by those of the King's younger subjects who have remained faithful—his Heroes and Queens. Or the Rebels may not be dealt with until after the Climactic Moment, as more of a loose end in the Resolution. This may especially be true if the King literally dies, and the new leader must deal with the Rebels in the aftermath.

Although the more dualistic and simplistic relationship between the younger archetypes of Maiden, Hero, and Queen and their respective antagonists is valid and important, the King Arc can be a good choice if you're wanting to explore a different take on "good versus evil" in your stories. The King's increasingly complex relationship with his antagonists offers much grist for thematic exploration.

Examples of the Cataclysm and Rebel Archetypes

Examples of the Cataclysm and Rebel archetypes include the following.

Cataclysm

- The Blip in *Avengers: Endgame*
- Grendel's Mother in *Beowulf*
- World War II in *Casablanca*
- The English in *Braveheart*
- Voldemort in *Harry Potter and the Deathly Hallows*
- The kaiju in *Pacific Rim*
- Jadis the White Witch in *The Lion, the Witch, and the Wardrobe*

Rebel

- Erik Killmonger in *Black Panther*
- Robert the Bruce in *Braveheart*
- Richard Cameron in *Dead Poets Society*
- Chuck Hansen in *Pacific Rim*
- Edmund Pevensie in *The Lion, the Witch, and the Wardrobe*

"A small piece of truth:
I do not carry a sickle or scythe.
I only wear a hooded black robe when it's cold.
And I don't have those skull-like
facial features you seem to enjoy
pinning on me from a distance.
You want to know what I truly look like?
I'll help you out.
Find yourself a mirror while I continue."
—Markus Zusak

27

DEATH BLIGHT AND TEMPTER

AS THE FIFTH of the six archetypal character arcs in the life cycle, the Crone Arc offers the first great challenge of a character's elder years. Fundamentally, it is a story about a character coming to grips with the full magnitude of mortality. Indeed, Death itself is the primary archetypal antagonist within a Crone Arc—or at least seems to be.

As noted in previous chapters, the protagonist's view of the archetypal antagonists evolves right along with her progression through the life arcs. What begins as a decided "me vs. them" viewpoint in the earlier arcs becomes increasingly more complex. By the time the character is challenged to decide whether or not she will "fight" that greatest of enemies—Death itself—she will surprise herself with the realization that perhaps Death is no enemy at all.

This, however, is a realization for the Climax of a Crone Arc, when finally she is able to move into the Liminal World. Throughout most of her story, the Crone's antagonistic forces are represented more specifically as a Death Blight and as the subtle Tempter who would lure her away from the Truth.

You may remember from Chapter 6 that the Crone begins her story feeling rather played out. Having just completed her King Arc, in which she nobly sacrificed her temporal power and position (i.e., her "life" in its previous guise), she may now believe the best part of her life is over and that she might just give in to the somnolent lure of a well-earned retirement. Her primary challenge is that of surrendering to her mortality—to Death—and in so doing resisting the temptation to wage war against Life out of her bitterness that it should be so. She is inspired to begin bringing her story full circle by fostering new Life, via the young of her Kingdom who still desperately require her wisdom and initiatory powers.

The Crone Arc begins to become more symbolic and metaphoric than any of the previous arcs. This is because, ultimately, her journey is an internal one. Her experience of the forces of Death, Life, and Temptation are ultimately all within. These antagonistic forces can, and probably will, be externalized as entities within the plot. But the true power and threat they represent is still something projected onto them from within the Crone herself.

The Crone's Antagonists: Practical and Thematic

Crone Arcs can be wildly fantastic adventures. But they are just as often quiet stories of internal contemplation, peopled with only a few supporting characters. Either way, it is useful to remember the external plot will be driven by a "practical" antagonist—one who creates specific obstacles to the protagonist's ultimate plot goal. Here, this external antagonistic force is the Death Blight.

Meanwhile, the Tempter may or may not be personified. If he or she is represented by an actual character, this character is often one of the most literal presentations of the contagonist, an antagonistic character who does not start out obviously aligned with the story's main antagonistic force. This character may oppose different facets of the protagonist's plot goal, or may even seem (and indeed may literally be) an ally. The crux of the relationship, however, is that the contagonist is *not* aligned with the protagonist's ultimate thematic Truth and will consciously or unconsciously tempt the protagonist away from that Truth and back into the Lie.

Often in a Crone story, the Death Blight and Tempter will seem integrally related, even if they are not in the end. Therefore, it can be easier than in other types of stories to purposefully blur the lines between the two, depending on how specifically they are represented in the story (i.e., by other characters).

The Death Blight as Archetypal Antagonist

Not to be too glib, the Crone's great lesson is that maybe Death isn't so bad after all. Or, more seriously, that Death and Life are not separate, that indeed they cannot be. To be in love with Life is to accept Death; to live a good life is to surrender to Death. And vice versa, to embrace Death is to embrace Life utterly.

This, however, is the Truth the Crone finds by the *end* of her story. What prompts her to take this journey in the story's beginning is a seeming Death Blight upon the Kingdom. And *this* face of Death seems anything but Life-affirming.

Although ultimately signifying nothing more than the Crone's own limited view of Life and Death, the Death Blight may be externally represented in the story in many different ways. It may be represented by limiting aspects of old age, such as illness or controlled living circumstances (e.g., being forced to move to a retirement home).

It can also be portrayed via unhealthy patterns shown in younger characters. Because the Crone's most frequent relationship character is often a young Maiden or Hero whom she initiates, the Death Blight may show up in the lifestyle of an unhappy teen embracing some form of "death culture" (such as drugs or other destructive patterns).

The Crone might also face high stakes in the broader world—an actual Death Blight of some kind descending upon the larger setting of her Kingdom. It could be she is not the only Elder who is being threatened by tyrannical younger characters but that she is the one to accept the journey into the Crone Arc in defense of the others. Or she may face an evil spirit of the land or culture that is poisoning the healthy evolution of younger archetypes. And, of course, she may face large-scale embodiments of malignant Death, via war or even something fantastical such as a zombie apocalypse.

Regardless, the antagonist she is ultimately facing is not Death in its true nature, but rather an *imbalance* of Life and Death. This could be because the prevailing culture has embraced Death in some violent way (such as in Nazi Germany), or it could be because the culture has rejected Death and refused, as the Crone is now being asked to do, to confront and embrace Death's natural and beautiful function.

The Tempter as Archetypal Antagonist

The Tempter may be merely an internal voice within the Crone's own head—seducing her into the notion that there is power to be had over Death or in resisting it. As often, however, the Tempter will be an externalized character. This character may be an "ally" of the Crone, urging her to reject her growing understanding of the importance of Death. Alternatively, the character may, in fact, be the orchestrator of the Death Blight, or at least someone who thinks they are able to control this malignant force.

Because the Crone is, symbolically, quite a powerful character, this Tempter is often represented by an equally or even more powerful character, such as the aggressive shadow version of the Mage—the Sorcerer. As such, the Tempter is a character who can be used to represent the dark potential in the Crone herself should she heed his sugared words or tempting example.

In Pixar's *Up*, we see the Tempter represented by the character of Charles Muntz. The protagonist Carl has idolized this mysteriously vanished explorer all his life, but Carl does not encounter Muntz until his elder years. Only then does he slowly begin to realize Muntz has turned malignant in his rejection of Death and his own mortality and now threatens the beautiful Life of the very rainforest he once championed.

Whether the Tempter is "master" or "servant" to the Death Blight, his primary function in the story is that of trying to unleash and harness the Crone's own potential for blighting the Kingdom.

How the Death Blight and the Tempter Operate in the Conflict and the Climactic Moment

The Death Blight will represent the external conflict and its main problem in some way. It could be that this problem literally grapples with questions of Life and Death. It could also be that the Death Blight's manifestation is merely a metaphor for the Crone protagonist's inner evolution into a new and broader perspective about the importance of this final act of her life. In facing the obstacles created by the Death Blight, the Crone will simultaneously be asked to face her fear of and resentment toward her own mortality.

The Tempter, meanwhile, may be represented merely by the Crone's own inner conflict *or* by a primary relationship character *or* by an obvious antagonist who is "creating" the circumstances of the Death Blight. What is important in regards to the Tempter is that he or she (or it) does in fact offer a legitimate temptation. The more powerful the Tempter's argument, the more powerful will be the Crone's ultimate transformation.

Depending on the nature of the story, the Death Blight may not be defeated in the Climactic Moment but instead redeemed or healed. The Blight aspect is removed and what remains is just Death—and Life. The Tempter may be entirely bypassed in this process. If the Tempter was "slave" to the Death Blight, then he will likely be destroyed in its absence. If the Tempter was "master," causing and wielding the Blight, then he will either be directly defeated or simply stripped of his power through some clever (and surrendered) move on the Crone's part.

However, it is always possible that little to nothing changes in the outer plot in the Climactic Moment of a Crone story. Because the thematic grappling with Life and Death is ultimately something that happens *within* the Crone, it is her final internal Truth that matters. Her acceptance, surrender, and inner peace is the final victory in her story, no matter the external trappings of the conflict.

EXAMPLES OF THE DEATH BLIGHT AND TEMPTER ARCHETYPES

Examples of the Death Blight and Tempter archetypes include the following.

Death Blight

- The war in *Howl's Moving Castle*
- Alzheimer's disease in *The Iron Lady*
- Sauron in *The Fellowship of the Ring*
- Old age in *Secondhand Lions*
- Isolation in *Anne of Green Gables*
- Old age in *Up*
- The Ghost of Christmas Future in *A Christmas Carol*
- Dinosaurs in *Jurassic Park*

Tempter

- The Witch of the Waste in *Howl's Moving Castle*
- Denis Thatcher's ghost in *The Iron Lady*
- Saruman in *The Fellowship of the Ring*
- Ralph and Helen (great nephew and niece) in *Secondhand Lions*
- Rachel Lynde in *Anne of Green Gables*
- Charles Muntz in *Up*
- John Hammond in *Jurassic Park*

"For evil in the open is but evil from
within that has been let out.
The main battlefield for good is not
the open ground of the public arena
but the small clearing of each heart."
—Yann Martel

28

EVIL AND THE WEAKNESS OF HUMANKIND

IT IS APPROPRIATE that the final archetypal character arc of the life cycle—the Mage Arc—should be the one to finally confront the ultimate antagonist within the human experience. This is, of course, Evil, in all its manifold abstractions.

As the final arc, the Mage (which we discussed in Chapter 7) symbolizes the end of life and, presumably, its fulfillment. Because the Mage is such a powerful and rare personage, the mysteries of his arc are ones few writers ever personally embody. Even still, they are ones we all instinctively speculate about. It is in the speculating that we sometimes are fortunate enough to offer to ourselves and perhaps to our readers a glimpse of greater truths and possibilities.

By its very numinosity and mysteriousness, the Mage Arc creates the opportunity for its archetypal antagonists to be personified in many different ways. As noted throughout this section, the archetypal antagonists faced within the successive life arcs grow increasingly less dualistic and more abstract as we go. In the First Act of life, the Maidens and the Heroes necessarily defined "Evil" as "the other" whom they were resisting and from whom they needed to individuate. Indeed, they were therefore inclined to then insist that the very nature of "otherness" must indicate Evil.

By the time the Crone makes peace with Death, it rather seems there is no concept of Evil left to confront. But the wisdom of the Mage sees a bigger picture that, in the earlier arcs, could only be instinctively and incompletely grasped. Perhaps most surprisingly, what the Mage recognizes as Evil is not so much a vast and primal entity, but rather something comparatively "small"—the evil that is the destruction and unhealth in the hearts of humankind.

And so the antagonist the Mage faces, whether portrayed in metaphor or not, is ultimately one he himself *cannot* defeat. Indeed, the larger part of his arc is centered around the struggle of realizing that to exert his great power in taking control of the situation—and therefore robbing autonomy and choice from the younger denizens of the Kingdom—would be perhaps the greatest evil of all.

The Mage's Archetypal Antagonists: Practical and Thematic

More than any of the preceding archetypal character arcs, that of the Mage can be seen as a passing of the torch. As the final life arc, the Mage's story ends, whether literally or symbolically, with the Mage's departure from this world. In future, he won't be around, in any guise, to give the younger archetypes a helping hand. From now on, they're going to be on their own.

And so the great need represented by the Mage Arc is that of his somehow making sure the Kingdom will be okay in his absence—that the cycle of life will roll on, hopefully in health and goodness. His great and final challenge is that of resisting the temptation to control this outcome, knowing that to do so would be to intrinsically destroy that natural cycle anyway. If he did so, he would, in Jean de la Fontaine's poignant words, "meet his destiny on the road he took to avoid it."

Evil as an Archetypal Antagonist

Is there any antagonistic force so archetypal as that of Evil? However much symbolic nuance resides within archetypes, they are, by their very nature, simplistic. They are stark, without shades of gray or even moral complexity per se. And Evil, of course, always seems very stark indeed.

By its very starkness, the concept of Evil can sometimes be difficult to write about. These days, our post-modern minds may argue with one another about what constitutes Evil or even if it really exists. And yet conceptually, it continues to show up in our fictional dreamscapes over and over and over again.

Although Evil can be and often is personified through the undeniably destructive and imbalanced actions of certain individuals, we see it portrayed most explicitly in fiction as nameless, faceless monstrosities. For example, the horror genre is designed around representing faceless Evil in various guises. Serial killers are often masked, and monsters are often mindless and soulless. There is no explanation for Evil's actions; it is beyond reason or even motive sometimes.

Within the younger archetypal arcs, antagonists may often be *seen* as Evil (and indeed may truly be so), but they are still usually personified in some way. These arcs are more concerned with simple conflicts that offer clear winners and losers. Whatever the antagonistic manifestation, it will be defeated in the form of the protagonist's current "Lie." The end. All is well. The Kingdom can exist happily ever after.

But the very nature of the life cycle indicates this happily ever after is only true until a *new* antagonistic force interrupts the character's life in the form of a new "Lie" he or she must overcome.

Theoretically within this model of archetypal arcs, the Mage represents the finality of the cycle. Naturally, this is not literally true, both because this cycle is but one possible archetypal exploration of life and also because infinite concepts such as archetypes can have no truly finite ends (no matter how much fiction would like to make it so). Nevertheless, within this model, the Mage represents the fulfillment of the cycle and therefore an ultimate showdown with the single great Antagonist who has in fact been represented in *all* the limited mindsets overcome throughout previous arcs.

The Evil the Mage faces may be represented as a great force that threatens the Kingdom, such as we find in so many fantasies and most notably with the Great Eye of Sauron in *The Lord of the Rings*. Even if this force employs a mortal army (as with Sauron's legions of orcs), the force itself represents an infinitude of some kind. More specifically, in its effects, it is usually recognized by the fact that it would eliminate free choice. In fantasy, it may literally do this by mind-slaving people; in more practical fiction, it may either exert a powerful tyranny and/or kill people—robbing them of any choice at all.

Therefore, we can see how Evil need not always be presented on a grand scale. If your Mage character is Gandalf the White, he will of course require a grand theater of metaphor in which to operate. But if your character is to appear in realistic fiction, then the Evil he faces can be as realistically "small" as simply the potential corruption infecting the heart of one single being—such as what Will Smith's titular Mage character faces in the heart of Matt Damon's character in *The Legend of Bagger Vance*.

Human Weakness as an Archetypal Antagonist

"Evil" is a very big word—and a very big antagonist. So perhaps it is surprising that in many Mage stories, this Evil manifests in the smallest of ways—not even in an obviously "evil" person, but simply in an ordinary person's weakness (or what Elder character Queenie in *Larkrise to Candleford* calls "hoo-man frailty").

This weakness is most poignantly obvious not in the hearts of the Mage's "enemies," but in the hearts of those very youngsters he loves and would mentor—the Maidens, Heroes, Queens, Kings, and even Crones whom he is about to leave behind. The Mage's great challenge is not to use his accumulated life's power to destroy the Evil, but rather to avoid the temptation of turning himself into that very Evil by taking away control—free will—from these younger, weaker characters.

In a triumphant Mage Arc, his very example and his great

WRITING ARCHETYPAL CHARACTER ARCS | 335

wisdom will be enough to inspire positive and necessary change in his wards. It is not the Mage who defeats the Evil in the end, but those in the Kingdom who have overcome the weakness in their own hearts. To the degree the Mage tries to protect the younger characters from facing the full conflict, or to the degree he attempts to control or manipulate their choices, he *becomes* Evil. And because he is a supremely advanced and powerful archetype, this fatal weakness in his own human heart would prove more dangerous than whatever Evil he resisted in the beginning.

How Evil and the Weakness of Humankind Operate in the Conflict and the Climactic Moment

Depending on how you choose to represent Evil as an antagonist within your story, you may emphasize it either as a huge and overwhelming "force" or as a much smaller conflict within a single relationship. There is the opportunity within the Mage Arc to either go really big and epic or really microscopic and intimate.

In a story that emphasizes Evil as a supernatural force, this force will usually motivate the external conflict. It may prompt a great war in which forces of Good and Evil oppose each other. And yet, even within the forces of "Good," the Evil will creep in on a more personal and interrelational level, as the Mage witnesses the weakness and temptation encountered by younger characters.

By contrast, a story that starts out emphasizing this potential for weakness within younger characters (and indeed the Mage himself) will usually focus more intimately on the consequences of the human characters' choices and actions. To the degree the Mage's influence fails—or to the degree the Mage himself manipulates the outcome—Evil will result in ways both large and small, creating plot obstacles and conflict.

For the Mage protagonist, the climactic encounter is less about defeating an enemy and more about surrendering to the end of the journey. Whether literally or metaphorically, he will step out of this mortal theater, leaving the younger archetypes to fight the battles they are meant to fight as they continue to progress through their own life cycles. Although not a protagonist, Master Oogway in the animated film *Kung-Fu Panda* offers a beautiful example of a character who fulfills all the best qualities of a true and positive Mage. With utter love but absolutely no attempt at control, he recognizes when it is time to leave the challenges of this life to those whom he has trained up behind him.

As noted, the Evil represented by antagonistic forces in a Mage Arc is really just "the Lie the Characters Believe." If the younger characters are able to manifest their own Positive Change Arcs and overcome their individual Lies from the respective stages of their own journeys, the Evil will be both defeated and transmuted. In exemplifying this, the Mage may not directly determine the end of the story's conflict, but he will at least initiate his beloved others to do so.

***

This now brings us to the end of our exploration of archetypal antagonists. Naturally, the twelve archetypal antagonists presented in this section are but a tiny fraction of possible archetypes to choose from in portraying your antagonist characters. However, these archetypal forces are the ones that create the practical and thematic conflicts for each of the archetypal character arcs discussed in Part 1. Even if you choose to use other archetypal antagonists in your stories, understanding how these forces integrally interact with life progressions can be helpful in crafting deeply resonant and cohesive fiction.

Examples of Evil and the Weakness of Humankind as Archetypes

Examples of Evil and the Weakness of Humankind archetypes include the following.

WRITING ARCHETYPAL CHARACTER ARCS | 337

Evil

- Lack of Christmas spirit in *The Miracle on 34th St.*
- Sauron in *The Lord of the Rings*
- Racism and prejudice in *To Kill a Mockingbird*
- The Matrix in *The Matrix*
- Selfishness and greed in *Mary Poppins*
- Loss of meaning in the wake of World War I in *The Legend of Bagger Vance*

Weakness of Humankind

- Doris and Susan Walker's skepticism in *The Miracle on 34th Street*
- Fear and cowardice in the hearts of Middle Earth in *The Lord of the Rings*
- Unjust judicial system in *To Kill a Mockingbird*
- People like Cypher who would prefer to return to enslavement in *The Matrix*
- Mr. Banks's inability to show love or understanding to his children in *Mary Poppins*
- Rannulph Junuh's desire to give up on himself and life in *The Legend of Bagger Vance*

Part 5:
Practical Application of Archetypal Characters

> "We live with our archetypes,
> but can we live in them?"
> —Poul Anderson

29

How to Use Archetypal Character Arcs in Your Story

WE FIND OURSELVES nearing the end of our journey through the possibilities of archetypal character arcs. I hope, like me, you are enthralled and excited by the possibilities archetypes offer for bringing depth, resonance, and structure to your stories.

So now what? Now that you've studied the six possible Positive Change Arcs within the archetypal life cycle, as well as the possible shadow devolutions, Flat resting periods, and archetypal antagonistic forces, what do you do now? How can you apply these archetypal character arcs to your own stories in a practical way?

As with all of story theory, just by learning about archetypes, you have already osmotically collected tools and references that will now show up naturally in your writing. Indeed, learning the specifics of archetypes only enhances what is already instinctive, since this intuitive understanding is the entire essence and point of archetype. From here, you can use these archetypes and their arcs to actively plan, plot, and write your stories. The structural beat sheets provided for each of the Positive Change journeys (Chapters 2–7) are a good place to start if you're wanting to apply any particular arc to your protagonist.

In this final chapter, we will close out the book with a short discussion of the more practical side of applying archetypal character arcs to your stories.

Finding Your Own Character Archetypes

First of all, let me encourage you to make these archetypes your own. Don't just take my word or the word of the many authors referenced throughout the book. Archetypes are resonant less because we mentally recognize them and more because we *feel* them. When we encounter a true archetype (or even just a subjective personal archetype), we feel the resonance deep within us.

When you experience this feeling, pay attention. It means you've almost certainly found something that matters to you and your life, and therefore probably something you should write about.

It's important to realize that archetypes are not necessarily fixed. The system presented in this book—as one I personally resonate with—is not the only system. There are many more archetypes than the ones I've discussed here. Want a Trickster in your story, or a Femme Fatale, or a Warrior? These archetypes can be explored in their own specificity and mined for equally exciting and important stories.

If this discussion of archetypes has connected with you, I highly recommend exploring the many books I've referenced throughout. A few are written specifically for writers; most are written for people interested in the human experience and in finding leverage points in their own personal development. None of these books present the life arc system exactly as I have, and almost all of them offer explorations of many different kinds of archetypes.

Here is a quick list of most of the books I've enjoyed on the subject:

- *The Hero With a Thousand Faces* by Joseph Campbell
- *The Heroine's Journey* by Gail Carriger
- *Women Who Run With the Wolves* by Clarissa Pinkola Estés
- *The Virgin's Promise* by Kim Hudson

WRITING ARCHETYPAL CHARACTER ARCS | 345

- *Walking on Water* by Madeleine L'Engle
- *King, Warrior, Magician, Lover* by Robert Moore and Douglas Gillette
- *The Heroine's Journey* by Maureen Murdock
- *Sacred Contracts* by Caroline Myss
- *The Hero Within* by Carol S. Pearson
- *Awakening the Heroes Within* by Carol S. Pearson
- *45 Master Characters* by Victoria Lynn Schmidt
- *The Writer's Journey* by Christopher Vogler

More than just reading and studying archetypes, look for them within yourself and your own experiences. Humans resonate with archetypes not because we find them outside ourselves, but because we recognize them as *part* of ourselves. Clarissa Pinkola Estés says it best:

> I encourage people to do their own mining of story, for the scraped knuckles, the sleeping on cold ground, the groping in the dark and the adventures on the way are worth everything. There must be a little spilled blood on every story if it is to carry the medicine.... I hope you will go out and let stories happen to you.

REMEMBER, ARCHETYPAL CHARACTER ARCS ARE DEVELOPMENTAL, BUT NOT ALWAYS LINEAR

Another important reminder is that although the archetypal system we have been studying is presented in a linear fashion, it doesn't have to be. Unlike the theory of plot structure and general character arc structure, these archetypal character arcs are not necessarily found in every story. They are not as strictly "episodic" in the sense that they should be told in a certain order and must be confined to one book at a time.

The structures I've suggested for each Positive Change archetype can be used for a single book, but it's also possible (although of course more complicated) to utilize multiple archetypes within the single structural character arc of one book. Although utilizing the archetypal character arcs in the presented order will make for a tidy, resonant, and sensible progression of character development—especially within a series—we all know real life isn't always so tidy. This is also important to realize when studying archetypes in other stories.

FIVE CONSIDERATIONS FOR HOW TO USE ARCHETYPAL CHARACTER ARCS

Are you ready to start writing epic archetypal stories? (I know I am!) What, then, are the best practices for applying these ideas to your own original works?

First of all, remember all these archetypal character arcs are built upon the foundational theories and practices of story structure and character arcs. A solid understanding of these ideas will help you immensely in then layering the archetypes on top. (You can learn more about these subjects in my books *Structuring Your Novel* and *Creating Character Arcs*.)

Second, don't forget that archetypal language is deeply and purposefully symbolic. None of it needs to be literal. In a fantasy story, you can *literally* use the archetypes if you wish, but you can also reach deep into the subtext of a hyper-modern and hyper-realistic story to find and utilize the same archetypes.

With these thoughts in mind, consider the following five pointers to help you start bringing archetypal characters to life in your fiction.

1. Identify Central Archetypes in Your Stories

The first step is, of course, to figure out which archetypal arc you want to explore in your story. You can do this in one of two ways. Either you can choose to tell a story about a Maiden, a Sorceress, a Ruler, etc., and then start constructing a plot around these ideas. Or you can examine an idea you already have for a story and determine which archetypes are naturally present.

For example, in plotting sequels to my own fiction, I soon realized the sequels were not (and could not be) another Hero

WRITING ARCHETYPAL CHARACTER ARCS | 347

Arc. The protagonist had already covered that ground and the sequels needed to progress the story. Realizing where the protagonist has already been is helpful in figuring out what comes next—and therefore which archetypes are likely to be the most accurate and useful.

2. Consider the Series as a Whole

If you're writing a standalone story, your considerations will be fewer: you need only choose a single archetypal arc to work with. But if you're writing a series, you can zoom out to consider the overall arc you will be crafting over the course of multiple books.

The archetypal life arcs neatly lend themselves to serial fiction. If you wish to tell the entire life's journey for a single character, you can easily do so by moving all the way through Maiden to Mage (with maybe some Flat Arc books in there about the Lover, Parent, etc.). If you know how large a story you intend to tell and where you want it to end up, you can better make room for all the necessary archetypal beats.

It's also possible to utilize a single archetypal arc (such as the Hero Arc) across the entire series, interposing the beats appropriately from book to book.

The clearer you are on this in the beginning, the easier it will be to create the necessary depth and resonance (and save yourself a lot of hassle).

3. Use Central Arcs to Choose and Flesh Out Supporting Characters

Once you've identified the archetypal character arc your protagonist will be taking—and therefore the archetype that will define the story—you can use this knowledge to flesh out a thematically solid supporting cast.

For example, if you know your protagonist will be following a Hero Arc, you will also know your story will benefit from supporting characters who represent the progressed archetypes of the King and the Mentor or the Mage. If you're writing a Queen Arc, you know your antagonist will have a double layer—both as the Invader who threatens the Kingdom and as the Puppet/Tyrant whose Empty Throne must be filled.

Particularly, you'll want to look for two types of supporting characters who can be represented archetypally:

> **1. Important Impact Characters**, represented by Flat archetypes, who will know the thematic Truth your protagonist is trying to grasp—and therefore will be able to offer guidance.
>
> **2. Antagonists**, who are symbolically important characters in all the Positive Arcs: Predator in the Maiden Arc, Dragon in the Hero Arc, Cataclysm in the King Arc, etc.

4. Pay Attention to Archetypal Themes

The thematic possibilities within your specific and individual archetypal stories are vast. Still, it's important to recognize that each archetype also offers inherent themes. To truly execute your personal themes well, you need to at least know what themes your chosen archetypes are representing.

In the first section of the book, I discussed the "core" thematic Lie/Truth for each archetype. Although you may choose to raise these Truths differently or to riff off their manifold nuances, at least be aware of the message the central archetypes will share with readers simply by existing within your story. (For more on finding your theme, see my book *Writing Your Story's Theme*.)

5. Mine Your Own Archetypal Experience

Inevitably, our stories are stories of ourselves—whether our past, present, or future. So consider how your own journey through the life arcs might impact your stories.

Where do you think you are within the cycle? Your age can give you a clue. If you are chronologically within the First Act (roughly, the first thirty years), Second Act (thirty to sixty years), or Third Act (sixty to ninety-plus years), you may not necessarily be on a corresponding life arc, but you will very likely be at least experiencing its call. Of course, because life

WRITING ARCHETYPAL CHARACTER ARCS | 349

isn't as neat as story theory, you may also find yourself chronologically in your Second Act but still cleaning up loose ends from First Act arcs, and so on.

Not only is this individual archetypal work personally and socially transformative, it is also deeply insightful for applying archetypes to your writing. Once you can see how you have experienced your own Maiden Arc or Hero Arc, you will be able to tap a vast storehouse of wisdom and understanding in writing these journeys for your characters—even if their stories take place in outer space or long-ago historical eras.

I will end with this challenge from Carol S. Pearson's *The Hero Within*, which speaks to the incredible potential offered to us by archetypes, both in our writing and in our lives:

> Systems theory tells us that when any element of a system changes, the whole system has to reconfigure. Therefore, simply by experiencing your own metamorphosis, you can contribute to the transformation of all the social systems of which you are a part: family, school, workplace, community, and society as a whole.

Thank you so much for joining me on the journey!

"Hope always draws the soul
from the beauty which is seen
to what is beyond,
always kindles the desire for the hidden
through what is constantly perceived.
Therefore, the ardent lover of beauty,
although receiving what is always visible
as an image of what he desires,
yet longs to be filled with
the very stamp of the archetype."
—Gregory of Nyssa

Appendix 1
Master List of the Archetypal Character Arcs

IN THIS APPENDIX, you will find an easy reference that lists comparisons of the six archetypal life arcs, so you can see them all in one place. Each of the individual chapters on the specific archetypes goes into much more depth and offers much more information, but this appendix should provide a handy overview, both to give you a zoomed-out look at the entire life cycle of the archetypes and also as a tool when you're trying to decide which archetype a character might be or which archetype is best suited to your particular story needs.

Remember: the arcs are not about *becoming* the central archetypes, but rather about reaching apotheosis and *transitioning out of* the height of that archetype's power into Death/Rebirth.

Overview of All Archetypes in the Life Cycle of Archetypal Character Arcs

Beginning Flat Archetype: Child

Maiden Arc
Shadows: Damsel (passive); Vixen (aggressive)
Subsequent Flat Archetype: Lover

Hero Arc
Shadows: Coward (passive); Bully (aggressive)
Subsequent Flat Archetype: Parent

Queen Arc
Shadows: Snow Queen (passive); Sorceress (aggressive)
Subsequent Flat Archetype: Ruler

King Arc
Shadows: Puppet (passive); Tyrant (aggressive)
Subsequent Flat Archetype: Elder

Crone Arc
Shadows: Hermit (passive); Witch (aggressive)
Subsequent Flat Archetype: Mentor

Mage Arc
Shadows: Miser (passive); Sorcerer (aggressive)

STORY TYPE FOR EACH ARCHETYPE

Maiden: An Initiation
Hero: A Quest
Queen: A Battle
King: An Awakening
Crone: A Pilgrimage
Mage: A Mission

ARC FOR EACH ARCHETYPE

Maiden Arc: Innocent to Individual (moves from Protected World to Real World)

Hero Arc: Individual to Protector (moves from Normal World to Adventure World)

Queen Arc: Protector to Leader (moves from Domestic World to Monarchic World)

King Arc: Leader to Elder (moves from Regal World to Preternatural World)

Crone Arc: Elder to Sage (moves from Uncanny World to Underworld)

Mage Arc: Sage to Saint (moves from Liminal World to Yonder World)

Symbolic Settings for Each Archetype

Maiden: Home
Hero: Village
Queen: Kingdom
King: Empire
Crone: Underworld
Mage: Cosmos

Thematic Lie vs. Truth for Each Archetype

Maiden: Submission vs. Sovereignty

"Submission to authority figures is necessary for survival." versus "Personal sovereignty is necessary for growth and survival."

Hero: Complacency vs. Courage

"My actions are insignificant in the overall scope of the world." versus "All my actions affect those I love."

Queen: Control vs. Leadership

"Only my loving control can protect those I love." versus "Only wise leadership and trust in those I love can protect them and allow us all to grow."

King: Strength vs. Surrender

"Physical strength is the pinnacle of human achievement." versus "Spiritual strength requires me to relinquish my physical strength."

Crone: Death vs. Life

"All life ends in death." versus "Life is Death and Death is Life."

Mage: Attachment vs. Transcendence

"My love must protect others from the difficult journey of life." versus "True love is transcendent and allows life to unfold."

Archetypal Antagonists for Each Arc

Maiden: Authority and Predator

Hero: Dragon and Sick King

Queen: Invader and Empty Throne

King: Cataclysm and Rebels

Crone: Death Blight and Tempter

Mage: Evil and the Weakness of Humankind

Archetypes' Positive Relationships to Own Shadow Archetypes

Maiden

> Damsel finally owns her Potential by embracing her Strength.
>
> Vixen learns to wield her true Potential with true Strength.

Hero

> Coward finally uses his Strength because he learns to Love and wants to defend what he loves.
>
> Bully learns to submit his Strength to the service of Love.

Queen

> Snow Queen finally acts in Love for her children by accepting Responsibility.
>
> Sorceress learns to submit her selfish Love to the greater love of Responsibility.

King

> Puppet finally wields his Power out of a growing Perception.
>
> Tyrant learns to submit his Power to the bigger picture of Perception.

WRITING ARCHETYPAL CHARACTER ARCS | 357

Crone

> Hermit finally accepts her Perception in order to grow into Wisdom.
>
> Witch learns to submit her Perception to the truths of greater Wisdom.

Mage

> Miser finally opens himself up through his Wisdom to gain Transcendence.
>
> Sorcerer learns to surrender his worldly Wisdom in exchange for true Transcendence.

Archetypes' Potential Relationships to Subsequent Shadow Archetypes as Represented by Other Characters

Maiden inspires Coward or outwits Bully with her inspiration.

Hero rescues Snow Queen or releases Sorceress with his love.

Queen empowers Puppet or overcomes Tyrant with her power.

King rallies Hermit or defeats Witch with his sacrifice.

Crone invigorates Miser or destroys Sorcerer through her wisdom.

Shadow Archetypes Overview

Damsel is Submissive (to avoid consequences of Dependence)

Vixen is Deceptive (aggressive use of Dependence)

Coward is Ineffectual (to avoid consequences of Courage)

Bully is Destructive (aggressive use of Courage)

Snow Queen is Defensive (to avoid consequences of Love)

Sorceress is Manipulative/Vampiric (aggressive use of Love)

Puppet is Irresponsible (to avoid consequences of Power)

Tyrant is Oppressive (aggressive use of Power)

Hermit is Misanthropic (to avoid consequences of Insight)

Witch is Punitive (aggressive use of Insight)

Miser is Selfish (to avoid consequences of Enlightenment)

Sorcerer is Evil (aggressive use of Enlightenment)

"Any legend, any creature,
any symbol we ever stumble on,
already exists in a vast cosmic reservoir
where archetypes wait.
Shapes looming outside our Platonic cave.
We naturally believe ourselves
clever and wise, so advanced,
and those who came before us
so naïve and simple...
when all we truly do is echo
the order of the universe, as it guides us."
—Guillermo del Toro

Appendix 2

How Story Structure and Archetypal Character Arcs Mirror Each Other

Patterns are everywhere in life. Story theory is no different.

As we've discussed throughout this book, story structure by its very nature is archetypal. It is a pattern we recognize emerging *from* story. It is a pattern as big as life itself, and therefore one about which we are always learning more, but also one we have been able to distill into specific systems that help us consistently recreate deeply resonant archetypes from story to story. When we study story structure and character arcs, we begin to realize these archetypal patterns show up in surprising ways.

The six primary archetypal character arcs we have explored in this book can be seen to make up the overall arc of a human life, beginning with the coming-of-age arc of youth and traveling all the way to the final challenges of confronting and embracing the mysteries of Life and Death. Not only do these innate journeys expand the options for archetypal journeys far beyond the beloved Hero's Journey, they also offer an amazing zoomed-out view of the common pattern of story structure itself.

Before closing out the book, I want to offer a side-by-side comparison of the six arcs next to the beats of classic story structure and touch upon how:

1. The cycle of the six archetypal character arcs shows us, as humans, how life itself is structured like a story.

2. The cycle also shows us, as writers, how the story structure in any individual book can be strengthened by recognizing that each of the classic structural beats mirrors specific archetypal chapters in life itself.

The Microcosm and the Macrocosm of Story Structure

Students of story have long been able to apply structure to their own lives and use it as a surprisingly accurate metric for recognizing archetypal moments and cycles. Once you understand the terms, it's hard not to see Inciting Events, First Plot Points, Moments of Truth, and Third Plot Points popping up all over the place.

More than that, once you factor in the archetypal arcs, you can reverse engineer these life beats into the structure of any individual story and use them to deepen the truly archetypal resonance of any particular beat. For example, when you begin to study the parallels between the Inciting Event in general and the Maiden Arc in the life cycle, both begin to take on deeper meaning.

Following is a quick overview of how story structure lines up with the archetypal character arcs. If you're unfamiliar with these ideas of story structure, you can find out more in my book *Structuring Your Novel*.

First Act

In story structure, the First Act represents the first quarter of the story or roughly the first 25%. It takes place in a familiar "Normal World" that, however wonderful (or not), is constricted by certain limiting beliefs. It is the place from which the character departs. It is the status quo to be changed.

From the perspective of the life arcs, the First Act can be seen to represent the first 20–30 years of the human life—

youth, in short. It is composed of the sequential Maiden Arc and Hero Arc, both of which are focused specifically on the character's learning how to individuate from the Normal World in which he or she grew up.

Inciting Event | Maiden Arc

In story structure, the Inciting Event is the first important structural beat within the story. It is the turning point, halfway through the First Act, taking place around the 12% mark. It is synonymous with what Joseph Campbell referred to as the Call to Adventure, in which the protagonist first "brushes" against the story's main conflict. The character will not yet leave the Normal World at this point, but she will, for the first time, glimpse the Normal World's limitations and see an opportunity for growing beyond it.

From the perspective of the life arcs, the Inciting Event equates with the Maiden Arc. This is the first of life's transformative archetypal character arcs, signifying the character's coming of age. Represented by puberty and the fraught years that follow, it is a "waking up" from the dream of dependent childhood into the realization that the world is much bigger. The Maiden Arc protagonist will not necessarily leave the physical Normal World within her story, but she will begin to individuate from her authority figures and caretakers so she *can* leave on her subsequent quest.

First Plot Point | Hero Arc

In story structure, the First Plot Point is the first of three major turning points. As the threshold or "Door of No Return" between the Normal World of the First Act and the Adventure World of the Second Act, it takes place around the 25% mark. This is where the protagonist fully engages with the main conflict. He leaves the comparative safety and familiarity of the Normal World in a way that, either literally or symbolically, means he can never return to the way things were. Everything has changed; the story is now fully underway.

From the perspective of the life arcs, the First Plot Point equates with the Hero Arc. Also an inherently youthful arc, this one follows sequentially on the heels of the Maiden's individuation and focuses on questions not just of independence but, eventually, of reintegration with a larger community. As he leaves behind all he has known and enters a strange and dangerous new world, the Hero focuses on questions of self-reliance, personal autonomy, and eventual responsibility. Although still operating mostly from the limited perspectives of his childhood, he begins now to confront the increasingly complex "real world" and its demands for him to balance his own needs with those of the greater good.

Second Act

In story structure, the Second Act represents the middle two quarters of the story, roughly from 25% to 75%. It takes place within the main conflict of the "Adventure World" and is focused entirely on moving the protagonist forward through a series of obstacles toward a final plot goal. These outer challenges will prompt the character's inner growth and transformation, increasingly broadening the character's perspective of life even to the point of altering his or her relationship to the plot goal itself.

From the perspective of the life arcs, the Second Act can be seen to represent roughly years 30–60 of the human life—or, adulthood. It is composed of the Queen Arc and the King Arc, both of which are focused on the character's relationship to others and to power. Between the two arcs, the Midpoint and its Moment of Truth changes everything, signaling a shift in focus from "acquiring" in the first half of life to "letting go" in the second half.

First Half of the Second Act | Queen Arc

In story structure, the First Half of the Second Act is traditionally a period of comparative "reaction." Having passed out of the Normal World through the Door of No Return in the First Plot Point, the protagonist has already taken a significant step into claiming her personal power. But she is also overwhelmed by the new challenges that face her, particularly since the worldview she brought with her out of the First Act limits her ability to understand and thus succeed in this new environment. Over the course of the First Half of the Second Act, the character will gather tools, resources, and allies that help her expand her understanding and move into a place of competence.

From the perspective of the life arcs, the First Half of the Second Act equates with the Queen Arc. Having returned successfully from the questing of the Hero Arc, the character is now represented by the Queen—a person of significant power and responsibility but one who is focused more on providing and nurturing than actually wielding that power. Her challenge is that of transitioning into true stewardship and leadership of her family/people. She summits in a powerful victory and takes the throne.

Midpoint | Moment of Truth

In story structure, the Midpoint and its all-important Moment of Truth takes place halfway through the story at the 50% mark, acting as a fulcrum for both plot and character arc. Here, the character glimpses the great Truth at the heart of his or her arc and begins to understand the conflict's bigger picture and therefore how to respond to it in a new and more effective way.

From the perspective of the life arcs, the Midpoint technically occurs *between* the Queen Arc and the King Arc. I see the Queen Arc as being more properly representative of the Midpoint's "Plot Revelation," which allows the character to upgrade her external efficacy in the plot. This can be seen in the Queen's rise to the throne. Meanwhile, I see the subsequent King Arc as being more representative of the Moment of Truth, when the character's relationship to the thematic principle alters through the understanding of a deeper Truth previously unavailable to him. This Truth evolves his tactics in the external plot, but more importantly it changes his understanding of the conflict's overall context and his own role within it.

Second Half of the Second Act | King Arc

In story structure, the Second Half of the Second Act is traditionally a period of "action." Having benefited from the lessons of the First Half of the Second Act and particularly its Midpoint, the protagonist now understands what to do better than he ever has before. Although still unable to fully relinquish limiting beliefs, he is now able to move through the conflict with much greater efficacy and empowerment. However, this ever-deepening understanding of the thematic Truth challenges almost everything the character thought he knew about himself, his plot goal, and the conflict itself. By the end of the Second Act, he will have to confront his darkest demons and discover whether or not he is honest enough to fully embrace his Truth.

From the perspective of the life arcs, the Second Half of the Second Act equates with the King Arc. The King Arc represents both the height of the character's temporal power and also the beginning of the end of that power. Confronted with deeper truths about the nature of Life and Death, the King must struggle between his desire for immortality and the practical need to begin releasing his power and passing the torch to the next generation. Now that he has seemingly gained it all, he must begin to let it go.

Third Act

In story structure, the Third Act represents the final quarter of the story, roughly from 75% through the end. It moves the protagonist into a final confrontation, both inner and outer, to determine whether or not the plot goal will be gained. Sometimes it will be gained; other times, the protagonist will choose to sacrifice the outer goal in order to maintain inner coherence with his or her newly learned thematic Truth. Although the story may end with the character's triumph, the Third Act is traditionally a period of darkness, temptation, and sacrifice, as the character struggles to choose between a Want and a Need.

From the perspective of the life arcs, the Third Act can be seen to represent the final or elder years of the human life—from 60 years and on. It is composed of the Crone Arc and the Mage Arc, both of which are focused on the final challenges of life, specifically the character's relationship to old age and death.

Third Plot Point | Crone Arc

In story structure, the Third Plot Point signals another threshold between Acts (another "Door of No Return" that mirrors that of the First Plot Point). It takes place around the 75% mark and is referred to by such dire terms as the "Low Moment," the "Dark Night of the Soul," and "Death/Rebirth." The events of the Third Plot Point emphasize what is at stake for the character now that she is this deep into the journey. So far, the character has risked much and gained much in the outer conflict, mostly thanks to the broadening of her perspectives into an alignment with the thematic Truth. But now, if the character is to succeed, she must finally and fully reject every last bit of the limiting Lie left over from the Normal World in the First Act. The person she was at the beginning of the story must die and be reborn into someone new. If the character can make that sacrifice, she can move on.

From the perspective of the life arcs, the Third Plot Point equates with the Crone Arc. More than any other of the life arcs, the Crone Arc is focused on the struggle against Death. It is the arc of old age, as the character confronts the loss of her temporal power and the looming approach of her mortality. Whether or not she can utilize a lifetime of growth in order to make peace with the nature of Life itself will determine much. She will journey to the Underworld and back to discover whether she can come into alignment with the Truths of her life or whether she will give up on herself—and everyone else—in despair.

Climax| Mage Arc

In story structure, the Climax begins halfway through the Third Act, around the 88% mark. It usually offers a series of scenes in which the protagonist confronts his final challenges. It ends with the Climactic Moment, which decides the story's conflict one way or another. In many stories, it is a segment of great excitement and tension. Most foundationally, it is a period in which the character puts to use all he has learned in the previous sections of the story. Is all he has learned truly true—or not? Has he truly changed—or not?

From the perspective of the life arcs, the Climax equates with the Mage Arc. Having overcome the terror and loneliness of the previous arc's Dark Night of the Soul, the Mage has transcended into great and often surprising spiritual power. Having successfully learned the lessons of all the previous archetypal arcs, he benefits from a truly broad and wise perspective of life. He moves through his final challenges and faces his final temptations as much for love of others as for himself.

***

Now, isn't that cool? I hope this comparison of how story structure aligns with the archetypal character arcs will help you deepen both plot structure itself and any of the archetypal journeys on which you decide to take your characters (or yourself).

Note From K.M. Weiland: Thanks so much for reading! I hope you've enjoyed learning how to use archetypes to strengthen your characters and stories. Did you know that reviews are what sell books? If *Writing Archetypal Character Arcs* was helpful to you, would you consider rating and reviewing it? Thank you and happy writing!

Want more writing tips?
CLAIM YOUR FREE BOOK!

Featuring some of K.M. Weiland's most popular tips on character crafting, this book offers a firm foundation for understanding the basics of character building, as well as solid tips for troubleshooting.

Discover inspiring quotes from successful authors, writing prompts, and creativity exercises. This book gives you the tools you need to tackle your latest batch of characters.

"Exactly the information and inspiration I was looking for to liven up my characters."

kmweiland.com/free-characters-book

REFERENCES

Aurelius, Marcus, *Meditations* (Sanage Publishing House, 2020)

Baldwin, James, *Conversations With James Baldwin*, edited by Standley, Fred L. and Pratt, Louis H. (University Press of Mississippi, 1989)

Bierce, Ambrose, *The Devil's Dictionary* (Bloomsbury USA, 2010)

Bolen, M.D., Jean Shinoda, *Crossing to Avalon* (Harper & Row, 1994)

Bolen, M.D., Jean Shinoda, *The Tao of Psychology* (Harper & Row, 1979)

Campbell, Joseph, *The Hero With a Thousand Faces* (Princeton University Press, 1949)

Carriger, Gail, *The Heroine's Journey* (Gail Carriger LLC, 2020)

Cather, Willa, *O Pioneers!* (Houghton Mifflin Company, 1913)

Donohoe, Sinéad, "How Not to Fall in Love With the Anima/Animus," <https://www.thereversegear.com/how-not-to-fall-in-love-the-animaanimus/>, September 29, 2016

Estés, Clarissa Pinkola, *The Women Who Run With the Wolves* (Ballantine Books, 1992)

Gardner, John, *The Art of Fiction* (Vintage Books, 1991)

Ghandi, Mahatma, *Ghandi: An Autobiography* (Beacon Press, 1957)

Hudson, Kim, *The Virgin's Promise* (Michael Wiese Productions, 2009)

Huntley, Chris and Phillips, Melanie Anne, *Dramatica* (Write Brothers Press, 1993)

Hurston, Zora Neale, *Their Eyes Were Watching God* (J.B. Lipping, 1937)

Jung, C.G., quoted in Bolen, Jean Shinoda, *The Tao of Psychology* (Harper & Row, 1979)

Koontz, Dean, *Velocity* (Bantam Books, 2006)

Lao-Tzu, *Tao Te Ching*, translated by Mitchell, Stephen (Harper and Row, 1988)

L'Engle, Madeleine, *Walking on Water* (WaterBrook Press, 1980)

Leonard, Linda Shierse, *The Wounded Woman* (Swallow Press, 1982)

Maass, Donald, *Writing 21st Century Fiction* (Writer's Digest Books, 2012)

Martel, Yann, *Life of Pi* (Mariner Books, 2002)

Meade, Michael, *The Genius Myth* (Greenfire Press, 2016)

Moore, Robert and Gillette, Douglas, *King, Warrior, Magician, Lover* (Harper Collins, 1990)

Murdock, Maureen, *The Heroine's Journey* (Shambhala Publications, Inc., 1990)

Myss, Caroline, *Sacred Contracts* (Harmony Books, 2001)

O'Brian, Patrick, *H.M.S. Surprise* (Williams Collins Sons & Co., Ltd., 1973)

Pearson, Carol S., *Awakening the Heroes Within* (Harper Collins, 1991)

Pearson, Carol S., *The Hero Within* (Harper Collins, 1986)

Rand, Ayn, *The Fountainhead* (Bobbs Merrill, 1943)

Rilke, Rainer Maria, *Letters on Life* (Modern Library, 2007)

Rothfuss, Patrick, *The Name of the Wind* (DAW, 2007)

Rowling, J.K., *Harry Potter and the Deathly Hallows* (Scholastic, 2007)

Schmidt, Victoria, *45 Master Characters* (Writer's Digest Books, 2001)

Shakespeare, William, *King Edward III*

Shreve, Anita, *The Pilot's Wife* (Back Bay Books, 1999)

Stark, Michael and Washburn, Michael, "Beyond the Norm: A Speculative Model of Self-Realization," *Journal of Religion and Health*, Vol. 16, No. 1 (1977)

Vogler, Christopher, *The Writer's Journey* (Michael Wiese Productions, 1998)

Whitman, Edward, quoted in Murdock, Maureen, *The Heroine's Journey* (Shambhala Publications, Inc., 1990)

Zusak, Markus, *The Book Thief* (Alfred A. Knopf, 2005)

Zweig, Connie and Wolf, Steve, *Romancing the Shadow* (Ballantine Books, 1997)

About the Author

K.M. WEILAND LIVES in make-believe worlds, talks to imaginary friends, and survives primarily on chocolate truffles and espresso. She is the award-winning and internationally published author of the popular writing guides *Creating Character Arcs*, *Outlining Your Novel*, and *Structuring Your Novel* (among others), as well as the gaslamp fantasy *Wayfarer*, the dieselpunk adventure *Storming*, and the portal fantasy *Dreamlander*. When she's not making things up, she's busy mentoring other authors through her award-winning blog Helping Writers Become Authors. You can email her at kmweiland@kmweiland.com.

Also by K.M. Weiland

Powerful Character Arcs Create Powerful Stories

Look deeper into the story beats that create realistic and compelling character arcs. Learn how to achieve memorable and moving character arcs in every book you write.

Take Control of Your Story Via a Powerful Implementation of Theme

When you learn to plan and implement theme, you will deepen your ability to write stories that both entertain and stay with readers long after the end.

Is Structure the Hidden Foundation of All Successful Stories?

Why do some stories work and others don't? The answer is structure. In this award-winning guide, you will discover the universal underpinnings that guarantee powerful plot and character arcs.

*Think being a superhero is hard?
Try being the first one.*

*Sometimes even pilots
have to wing it.*

What if dreams came true?

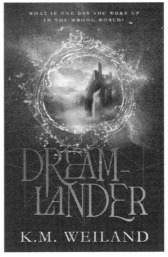

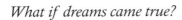

KMWeiland.com

All Books by K.M. Weiland:

Behold the Dawn

Dreamlander

Storming

Wayfarer

Non-Fiction

Outlining Your Novel

Outlining Your Novel Workbook

Structuring Your Novel

Structuring Your Novel Workbook

Creating Character Arcs

Creating Character Arcs Workbook

Writing Your Story's Theme

Jane Eyre: The Writer's Digest Annotated Classic

Conquering Writer's Block and Summoning Inspiration

5 Secrets of Story Structure

Acknowledgments

My profound thanks to the patrons of Helping Writers Become Authors!

Sherry A
Bill Abbey
Nigar Alam
Milla Alavuotunki
Anne Andersen
Amber
Philip H. Auerbach
Hussain Bassam
Tyson Beck
Denise Berndt
Melissa Blevins
E. G. Bertran
Evelyn Breithaupt
Bret
Kelly Brockett
Andrea Broumley
Carl Brown
Lois Brown
Andrew Burns
David Butler-Groome
Heather C. Cardona
Jackie Casey
James Christensen

Andy Clark
Carol Lea Clark
Terrence Cleary
desAnges Cruser
Della Curtis
Dahna Danli
David Darcy
Scott Davis
Kristen DeClemente
Usvaldo de Leon
Laredo Dixon
Stevie Rae Drawn
N. R. Eccles-Smith
MJ and Jesse Fanta
Anouchka Freybe
Megan Plank Gibbs
Cain Gonzales
GS
Debora Habsburg
Tresha Haefner-Rubinstein
Cynthia Sally Haggard
Natasha Hanova
Barberella Haymaker

Nala Henkel-Aislinn
Iliff Hicks
Rob Hill
AC Hoekwater
E R Hoffer
Jessica Hohmann
Carol Hubbard
Parker Hudson
invalidname
Jennifer
Dexter Jacobs
Joking611
Drew Jones
Elisabeth Kauffman
Larry Keeton
Renee Leonard Kennedy
Juneta Key
Alice Kindl
Jacqueline Kirk
Alina Klein
Zsolt Kovari
Tracey L
Peter Lakeshore
Milree Latimer
Diana Lawrence
Della Leavitt

Nicolas Lemieux
Suzanne Leslie
Tyrone Liggians
Lise
Jason L Lunday
William Henry Lyne
Peter Mackey
Mallika
William Marden
Marie
Marsha
CJ McCay
Meredith
Nathan Miles
Margaret A. Miller
Mon221B
Dragana Munitic
Meg Murray
Joseph Nastanski
Adrienne Nesiba
Jenny North
Travis O
Lyn Oakland
Shannon O'Hare
Kirstin Olson
Kris Partello

Katrina Pavlovich
David Penny
Anthony Pero
plebeianpenguin
Terri Pulley
Claude R.
David Ranghelli
Dave Reed
Bill Reid
Ashley Rescot
Janice Rickey
Craig Scott Roberts
Brian Rogoski
Jada Rowland
D.L.Ryder
Soleah Kenna Sadge
Julie Samms
Henrik Sannesson
Saskia
Ashley Shewmake
Louis Schlesinger
John Sheets

Skyman's Follies
Don Smallwood
Michael Smith
Nita Smyth
Sophia-Maria
ThatCoffeeLifter
Eric Troyer
Steve Tye
John Warfield
Dan Wathen
Joel Weddington
Marnie Werner
Derek Wheeless
Andrea Whitmore
Jessie Wilbanks
Katie Wilson
Daniel Wilton
Jerry Windley-Daoust
Sionnach Wintergreen
Donovan Wood
Miriam C Zaccarelli

Extra thanks to all the Wordplayers and especially Anthony Findora, Dave Gibbons, Cain Gonzales, Shannon Gonzales, and Joanna Marie for their generous help with beta reading and proofreading, as well as Joseph Merboth and Joseph Nastanski for their help with the back cover description.